THRILL SEEKERS

15
REMARKABLE WOMEN
in EXTREME SPORTS

ANN McCALLUM STAATS

Published by Chicago Review Press Incorporated
814 North Franklin Street
Chicago, Illinois 60610
ISBN 978-1-64160-480-2

Library of Congress Control Number: 2020951039

Cover, Illustrations, and Interior design: Sadie Teper

Printed in the United States of America

5 4 3 2 1

To everyone who was ever my student—you know who you are.

Contents

Introduction

What if you could:

Fly over trees and fields, soaring through the air as if you were a bird?

Swim underwater past dozens of thousand-pound sharks?

Spin off a snow-covered jump, rotating into a double flip and landing with perfect precision?

Unthinkable? Impossible? Not to the women in this book. These are women whose determination, grit, and courage have propelled each of them into lives of extraordinary risks and rewards. But what drives them? What makes Faith Dickey balance on a narrow band of webbing thousands of feet in the air? How does Kristin Knight Pace travel by dogsled through some of the coldest and most hostile wilderness on the planet? Does Brittany Leavitt ever think twice before she scrambles up a near vertical rock face with nothing but her own strength to power her to the top?

The women in this book are not superhumans, and they're not fearless. They experience doubts and are often uncomfortable, even afraid. The difference is that they have learned to assess their uncertainty. If there's a real and legitimate danger, they will make a rational decision to stop. However, being frightened of the what-ifs doesn't count. Instead, Bethany Hamilton will take on a killer wave, using its crushing force to surf a ride that is as exhilarating as it is life changing. Angela Hawse will trek to the top of the world's highest and most treacherous mountains to earn a breath of the most pristine air on earth. And Lizzie Armanto will attempt a mind-boggling kickflip, pushing aside the possibility of failure and going at it until she gets it right. How do they do it? And why? Maybe their motivation comes from achieving something that makes them feel ultra-alive—perhaps it's because *not* doing it would be like living life from behind a curtain.

Each of these action adventurers comes from humble roots. None had it easy, and none had lives without struggle and personal sacrifice. Yet each is an inspiration, a bull's-eye of audacity and bold resolve. To every reader of this book: Buckle up for a wild and thrilling ride. May you feel inspiration and awe as you pedal, vault, carve, run, fly, steer, and plunge your way through these real-life adventures.

What do *you* long to do? Three, two, one! Go for it!

Part I: Maximum Sky

Roberta Mancino:
Fly Like a Superhero

Roberta Mancino zipped the arms of her wingsuit closed, the thrill of what she was about to do causing her heart to beat faster. In just a few moments she would be jumping from the helicopter in the specially designed suit that would allow her to glide horizontally, the closest a human being could get to flying like a bird. With fabric "wings" stretched between her arms and legs, the increased surface area would allow her to soar for miles before having to deploy the parachute strapped to her back. She adjusted her goggles next, necessary to protect her eyes from the force of the wind—along with the sulfur-laced smoke infusing the air below her. Roberta was about to fly directly over an active volcano.

Villarrica is a classic cone-shaped mountain towering 9,341 feet (2,847 m) above sea level in Chile. When Roberta gazed at it from the open door of the helicopter, she noted that it was dotted with snow, though the top opened to a pit of glowing orange lava. If she could have measured its temperature, she would have found that this molten rock was over 1,000 degrees Fahrenheit (540°C). Not only that—since it was active, the colorful magma could spew upward at any time.

When Roberta first arrived in the country, the locals told her that Villarrica had another name. They called the volcano Rucapillán, a Mapuche word for "devil's house." Today's flight would be historic. Never before had anyone attempted to fly a wingsuit over Villarrica. Never before had a woman flown over *any* active volcano. Roberta's bright red wingsuit was equipped with cameras. She had one on her helmet along with another attached to the torso of her suit. Her team had cameras, too— they didn't want to miss recording a second.

The stunt was dangerous, but Roberta and her team had planned meticulously, like they always did, first securing permission from their host country and then calculating the many logistical issues that could affect the flight, such as wind speed and altitude. It would be a long glide, too. Roberta needed to get off the mountain and its lava fields and fly to a secure landing area in the rocky plain below. She had no reserve parachute with her; there was no point. By the time it was safe to land, it would be too late to deploy a second chute.

"Don't fly too close," one of the locals had advised her earlier. "Hold your breath for a few seconds when you go over the top." It was a reminder that the volcano was active and that the mountain was constantly discharging noxious gases and heat. But Roberta and her team had lucked out. So far, the volcano was calm that day. The weather conditions were perfect, too.

Roberta stepped outside the helicopter and balanced for a moment on a narrow platform built over the wheel. It was time. She dropped into the air, spreading her arms and legs to engage the wings of her suit. With wrists bent, she gripped the sides of the arm wings to keep them as rigid as possible. The heart of the volcano roiled red and orange below her, and turbulence from the terrific heat gave her extra lift. She was flying!

Roberta Mancino has received worldwide recognition as a model, skydiver, wingsuit flyer, and BASE jumper (BASE jumping is taking off from a stationary object on earth rather than jumping from an airplane or helicopter). Born on August 3, 1980, Roberta grew up in Anzio, Italy, about 30 miles (48 km) south of Rome along the coast. She had an active childhood, starting with dance classes at the age of four. Her training in classical ballet and Latin American salsa helped her later when she participated in freestyle skydiving, a subgenre of the sport that involves acrobatic maneuvers during free fall.

When she was 15, Roberta had her first boyfriend, a boxer who introduced her to his gym. There she tried boxing and kickboxing for the first time. It was just what her energetic body craved. Practicing for hours every day, she earned a black belt in mixed martial arts.

Roberta was swimming one day when a scout approached her and asked if she wanted to try modeling. She said yes and participated in her first modeling gig at the age of 16. It was fun, but it wasn't enough. Roberta continued to try different adventure sports such as scuba diving and paragliding. At her modeling sessions, the director would frown over the inevitable bumps and bruises on Roberta's body. As the team covered the marks with makeup, he admonished her, "No sports for two weeks before the next shoot."

But Roberta yearned for action, and she wanted to experience all life had to offer, the faster the better. She set her sights on skydiving when two friends showed her some online videos. They teased Roberta, "You're too little. You're too young." You had to be 18 to try it. And Roberta's mother had a message for the boys: "You're *not* taking her skydiving."

But of course, the moment she turned 18, Roberta signed up to go skydiving. Her first jump was in Italy, just outside Rome. When she showed up, there were only men in the course, mostly from the military. The system they were using was called a static line. She would jump solo, but there was a line connected to the airplane that would automatically pull open her parachute as it grew taut. "Of course, I was scared," Roberta recalled. "But I had waited so long. . . . I didn't have the attitude that I was going to do this just once. I knew I wanted to be a skydiver."

Roberta jumped. From that moment, she confirmed what she'd suspected all along. She had found her passion. Flying was a feeling like no other. The adrenaline rush, the speed, and the challenge to her body were all things Roberta loved—and couldn't get enough of.

"I feel free in the air," she said. "I love the feeling with my body flying in the air."

Once she had completed 6,000 skydive jumps, Roberta decided to try wingsuit flying. At first, she jumped from an airplane and found that the experience was not that much different from skydiving. Soon after, she took things a step further and tried BASE jumping.

BASE Jumping Through the Ages

People have been jumping from fixed structures for centuries. Inspired by Leonardo da Vinci's parachute sketch, many inventors modified his design and even tried it themselves—often ending in catastrophe. In 1783 Louis-Sebastien Lenormand successfully jumped from the tower of the Montpellier Observatory in France using a homemade parachute. Others followed, designing their own parachutes and finding new places to jump from. For example, while modern parachutes weigh about 20 to 25 pounds (9–11 kg), in 1912, Frederick Law jumped from the Statue of Liberty wearing a 100-pound parachute (and lived).

The birth of contemporary BASE jumping began with Carl Boenish in 1978. He coined the term that describes the four possible jumping-off points: buildings, antennas, spans (bridges), or earth features such as cliffs. The technique for leaping off one of these structures and landing safely requires a lot of expertise. Since the jumper has less time to deploy a chute than if she were in an airplane, timing is critical. Another danger is the proximity to where you start and the possibility of hitting something on the way down. For these and other reasons, BASE jumping is illegal in most cities.

Roberta didn't try BASE jumping until she had completed 200 wingsuit jumps from an airplane. She needed to be satisfied that she could successfully manage anything that went wrong. It was one thing to jump from a plane, wait for the requisite altitude, and then pull a chute. It was another thing to start from a cliff, jumping far enough away to clear any protruding rock, and then fly horizontally, maintaining control at a terrific speed until it was time to deploy the parachute close to the ground.

The first time she tried it, Roberta was scared. She knew she could die, but she wanted to try flying more than she feared the risk. After all, it was a chance to experience flight like a bird. In free fall from a plane, it wasn't obvious how fast you were going. When flying along the edge of a cliff in a wingsuit, you could track the scenery beside you as well as below you. This bird's-eye view provided much more awareness of speed and distance. She had been dreaming of flying, really flying, since she was a kid. Now was her chance.

Roberta adjusted her gear one last time. She was perched on a cliff at Brento, a favorite BASE location in Italy. As she checked her helmet and the strap across her chest, she ran through the safety features of her equipment. Her helmet had a reinforced chin guard. There were hand and leg straps on her wingsuit to keep the wings securely in place. The heavy-duty zippers were tough and would not rip. Roberta hesitated a moment longer, surveying the vista before her—and the 4,000-foot (1,220 m) drop. Then she was off.

Fly Like a Bird . . .

. . . or a flying squirrel. As soon as a wingsuit flyer jumps from a plane, helicopter, or high object, she must engage the anti-rip material stretched between the legs, arms, and torso of the suit. This webbing inflates through tiny slits in the fabric and forms three semirigid wings. As soon as a flyer jumps, the wingsuit makes use of this increased surface area to fight against gravity. Wearing a wingsuit allows a person to soar for long distances, while descending at a speed of about half that of skydiving. The forward speed, meanwhile, can be 100 miles per hour (160 kph) or more. A flyer can also maneuver in the air using small, controlled movements (large movements can result in dives or wild spins). To land, a wingsuit flyer must deploy a parachute to slow her velocity and transition back to earth.

Once Roberta had experienced wingsuit flying, she couldn't get enough of it. She racked up more and more jumps, some still from airplanes or helicopters, but others from beautiful cliffs and mountains. Each time, she loved emulating the flight of a bird. Roberta was in Dubai when she first wondered what it would be like to fly in a city. As she looked up, the tops of the skyscrapers beckoned to her. However, when the United Arab Emirates' officials denied her request to try BASE jumping there, she set her sights on another urban setting. Soon she was planning a wingsuit flight in Panama City, Panama.

For the Panama City flight, Roberta wore a shimmery white wingsuit with a matching helmet studded with diamond-like sequins. She had cameras on her suit and a partner who would fly nearby to record the flight as well. After going through her regular safety routine, she secured the strap on her helmet and stepped out of the helicopter. Her path was straightforward— she would fly over the water to the coastline. From there she would aim for a gap between twin skyscrapers. She needed precise flying to clear the space between the buildings, but she wasn't worried. There was plenty of room. What she didn't count on was the beginning of a storm and the terrific crosswinds that unexpectedly popped up between the buildings.

In the video, viewers see Roberta in her suit heading toward the buildings. She clears the left skyscraper by tilting her suit. What you don't see is the air turbulence that could have easily caused her to crash into the building. "The wind was picking up and that's why on the video you can see my face at one point . . . as soon as I pass the buildings I just kind of scream. I got scared because I didn't expect such push from the crosswind," Roberta said. "That's OK *after* you pass the buildings and there's nothing there, but you don't want that to happen when you're in between."

Dream of Flying

Throughout history people have looked to the sky, envying birds who swoop and dip and soar seemingly effortlessly. From earliest times, various attempts to mimic this natural flight have proven difficult—sometimes fatal. Skydiving and BASE jumping predate wingsuit flying. Before wingsuit flyers, BASE jumpers leaped from an earth-anchored object to deploy a parachute—falling rather than flying. The wingsuit changed all that. Despite the danger, innovators and risk-takers continued to experiment until finally, in the late 1990s, two European men tested a prototype of what would become the first commercially available wingsuit. With horizontal momentum, wingsuit flyers can descend at an average rate of 3:1, meaning that for every three feet of forward movement, there is a one-foot drop. Today, wingsuit flyers have sped faster than 240 miles per hour (390 kph), flown over 9 minutes, and traveled nearly 20 miles (32 km). One man, Gary Connery, landed without deploying a parachute. Instead, he cushioned his fall with a landing zone made from thousands of empty cardboard boxes—and survived.

Earning more and more recognition for her work, Roberta was part of a team that was approached by Hollywood. Would she be interested in performing a stunt that would require meticulous planning and precision flying? *Of course,* thought Roberta. *That's what I always do.*

The scene was for the upcoming *Iron Man 3* movie. In it, the script called for 13 passengers plus Iron Man himself to be flung out of an airplane—Air Force One—after it was blown up midair. Iron Man would save the passengers by having them "link up" and then drop into a lake below. The movie staff wanted to do as much of the scene as possible with real people and real actions, rather than computer-generated imagery (CGI). Roberta and the others would play the passengers, and they would have to pretend to be falling out of control before connecting haphazardly in a highly technical formation skydive. The scene was dubbed the "Barrel of Monkeys" segment because Iron Man appears to gather up the tumbling passengers, who then connect themselves together like in the old-fashioned game of plastic monkeys.

On the set of the Iron Man movie, it felt like a dream. *Wow. Wow. I'm doing this for real!* Roberta told herself, resisting the urge to pinch her arm to see if she was awake. She was a huge fan of Marvel comics, and here was a chance to look into the moviemaking behind the superheroes that were so much fun to watch. The project itself was hectic. The scene involved six days of filming and while some of it was digitally created, almost all of it was real, live-action work.

Each day, the team made up to eight jumps. They wore costumes, business-style clothing that had been designed to hide parachutes underneath. Roberta strapped on high heels, securing them so they wouldn't blow off. Then, as the team exited their aircraft at about 12,000 feet (3,660 m), they pretended to be plummeting out of control. Roberta's role was to crash into Iron Man. "Crash a little harder next time," the stunt manager told her. *No problem*, Roberta thought. She might get a few bruises, but she knew what she was doing. Besides, it was fun!

The next part of the stunt involved building a complicated skydive formation that was carefully orchestrated to look chaotic. The final shot, where Iron Man decelerates so he can drop the people harmlessly in the water, required a different technique. For these final moments of the scene, the team was attached by wires to a giant crane. The crane swung the group over the water before releasing a couple of people at a time. When Roberta watched the scene in the movie, it appeared as if Iron Man was holding onto the connected group and then dropping them into the water. It looked real. It looked fantastic!

Hollywood Lights

Crash! Leap! Burn! While there is no formal degree required to be a stunt person, it takes a lot of practice and experience to get work. In addition, all stunt performers in the United States must be members of a special actors' union. This ensures that all safety protocols are taken in what can often be a dangerous profession. Once a person does find work, it takes practice, practice, practice. Whenever a stunt scene is created, every detail is carefully planned and rehearsed many times before anything risky is introduced. For just a few moments in a film, stunt people might need to work for days to get everything just right.

Roberta had logged over 10,000 skydives and more than 450 BASE jumps when she signed a contract to star in Nissan's "Freedom to Move" commercial. The opening scene of the commercial shows Roberta driving the electric car along a winding road. Suddenly, a cutaway shows Roberta in her wingsuit, launching from the high road, spinning in the air, and maneuvering through the city. She flies past a parking garage, between two buildings, and along an inner-city road. While a lot of this is staged and computer-generated, it was another adventure in Roberta's exciting life.

Whether she is under contract or whether she is flying for herself, Roberta feels most at home in the air. "I feel good there. . . . Up there, everything is beautiful. You can just fly with no bad experience." It's on the ground where Roberta feels weighed down. There you can find plastic in the ocean, sickness, and everyday dangers, such as scary traffic or bad people. She says, "It scares me sometimes to be on the ground."

However, Roberta still reflects on the uncertainty she has often felt before trying something new. She admits that she has felt afraid many times: "It's good to be scared. At the same time, be determined." She elaborates, "You can be scared and do nothing. Or, you can fight it and don't be so afraid." Roberta smiles. "You have to have courage."

Today, Roberta's life is fast-paced and exhilarating. As she plans a wingsuit jump to drop her mother's ashes over the Dolomites in Italy, she has signed contracts for other movies and projects.

Roberta doesn't see her life grounded anytime soon. Not if she can help it.

Follow Roberta Mancino Online

Instagram: @mancinoroberta
Twitter: @Roberta_Mancino
Facebook: Mancino Roberta
YouTube: www.youtube.co/user/robertamancino

Faith Dickey:
Walk a Thin Line

Imagine walking in a perfectly straight line, one foot exactly in front of the other. Imagine that line is above the ground, and it is a one-inch, flat, woven band that is not taut, but stretchy and dynamic, bouncing and swaying with every step you take. This is slacklining. If it's high off the ground, sometimes hundreds of feet up or more, it's called highlining.

The first time Faith Dickey saw a slackline anchored between two pecan trees in a park in her native Austin, Texas, home, she thought, "That's impossible. That's way too hard." Never mind that Faith went on to be the first woman to walk a 100-meter (328-ft) highline. Never mind that she earned several world records that went unchallenged for years, or that she has walked highlines dozens of times without a safety harness. During that initial experience, Faith had no idea that someday she would be a professional highliner, or that she would build control over her fear and be able to share that insight with others.

That day in the park, Faith was 19 years old. A recent high school graduate, she had a careful and distinct plan for her life. Juggling five part-time jobs, her life was unbelievably busy. Faith worked up to 80 hours a week, focusing on saving enough money so she could move to New York City to study fashion design. When she saw that first slackline, she was intrigued, despite her doubts. She tried walking along the narrow band, but immediately fell off, thankful that it was only a few feet off the ground.

When she left the park, she wondered what kind of inner focus and intense concentration it would take to actually make it the entire way across the narrow line. But those thoughts didn't linger too long. With her multiple jobs and dream of moving to New York, she really didn't have time to find out.

One defining moment helped change the course of Faith's life. Exhausted and ragged from working nearly nonstop, Faith fell asleep while driving her car. The vehicle flipped over and was completely destroyed. Although she wasn't seriously injured, the accident shook Faith up in a way that she had never experienced before. The path she had so carefully planned for her life was now out of focus. Suddenly, she realized she wasn't ready to rush off to New York to pursue a career in fashion design. Instead, she quit half her jobs and started spending more time in the park, coming back again and again to the slackline.

Unsure of what she wanted to do next, Faith felt the tug of something more. She used her small savings to purchase a one-way ticket to Europe. She brought along her own slack-line equipment to continue practicing the new sport she had fallen in love with. There, she happened upon a slackline festival taking place in Germany. When she got there, she noticed a line stretched 50 feet (15 m) above the ground instead of the few inches she was used to. She watched in amazement as others traversed this highline strung between a water tower and a building. Faith decided to try it for herself.

It was intense! Someone showed her how to wear a harness with a leash that would be clipped to the line behind her. Once she strapped on the safety gear, Faith climbed up and stood at the edge of the highline. *Oh man, if I don't do this right I could kill myself.* She was gripped by a nearly paralyzing fear.

Her body shook as she tried to walk across the narrow webbing—and fell. Now she was dangling below the line. It took enormous strength to climb the rope to get back up. She tried more times. And fell, again and again. The voice of fear kept nipping at her, crushing her confidence and gnawing away at her focus. She told herself, *I'm not cut out for this.* Gradually, though, Faith's fear transformed into determination. It was still scary, but after multiple falls wearing the harness, she knew she was safe.

Faith met a couple of guys at the festival and they teamed up, giving themselves a name: the "Somewhereelseland." Traveling from one slacklining event to another, over and over Faith failed to walk an entire line without slipping off. Still, attached to her leash and hanging below each line, she knew she was going to keep trying. She told herself that it was important to fall in order to reinforce the fact that she was safe. The mental aspect of the sport was just as big a hurdle as the physical part—maybe bigger. Faith found that walking a highline was terrifying, but somehow also freeing. Thoroughly hooked on the sport, she set her mind on getting better.

Rigging a Line

Setting up the rigging for a highline is a complex and multifaceted operation. In never-before-highlined areas, bolts have to be drilled into the rock (if it's legal). Each end of the line has three to five bolts embedded into the rock. A team must secure the line to each one of the bolts, ensuring that the tension is distributed equally and that it provides a stable anchor. In some places drilling bolts is against the law. If that's the case, Plan B is to fasten the rope around features in the landscape such as an outcropping of rock. That way there is no damage to the rocks. This approach is much more complicated and requires creative problem solving according to the terrain. Either way, rigging a highline requires a lot of time and effort. It can include a strenuous hike to the chosen spot, climbing to the top of a rock formation or mountain, and then spending hours preparing the anchors for the highline—and checking them multiple times.

The first time Faith successfully walked across an entire highline, she was in Poland. It was on a brand-new line, between two rocky outcroppings and in a place where nobody had ever rigged a line before. Her teammate, now her boyfriend, suggested she try it first. It was a huge honor to have the first attempt at an untried highline. Fighting to tame her fear, to control her focus, and to concentrate on the moment, Faith walked the whole way across without falling. She was ecstatic! She had worked so hard for this success, trying harder than anything else she had ever attempted. She felt a sense of freedom and empowerment she had never felt before.

As the team continued to rig lines and practice highlining, Faith came to another crossroads. With a "passionate addiction to balance," she realized that she could make highlining her life, but she would need to quit everything else and concentrate on just it. With her small crew, she began finding sponsors while participating in the sport at every opportunity. As she practiced, Faith got better. Much better. She learned how to fall so that she grabbed the line rather than let the leash catch her. She taught herself to sustain intense attention to the moment, a critical aspect of walking a highline sometimes thousands of feet in the air—her personal record was a highline 4,000 feet (1,220 m) above the valley floor in the Swiss Alps.

Like most people, Faith has a human measure of fear. She is afraid of "regular" things like sharks and spiders and financial instability. She definitely does not have a death wish. Yet acknowledging fear was critical to her success. This emotion, she learned, was the biggest inhibitor to her victory in the sport. If she stepped onto a highline and her mind was racing with the negative possibilities of her situation, this panic could derail her—literally. She found that no matter how many times she proved to herself that she could physically accomplish something, the mental part was still the biggest challenge. She trained herself to logic each situation out:

Am I safe? she would ask herself. *Yes.*

Do my teammates want me to succeed? Yes.

Can I walk this line? Yes.

Faith focused on her mental training and developing excellent stamina. Besides using reason to tamp down the fear, Faith would also visualize success. If she could accept the risk and focus only on the act of stepping one foot by one foot to the other side, she could minimize the mental barrier that whispered defeat. Whenever she reached the end of a highline, she felt relief, of course, but also a huge level of freedom and empowerment that she hadn't experienced in other areas of her life.

What About Safety?

Like any sport, in highlining a progression of steps ensures maximum safety. First is the equipment itself. The key to minimizing the likelihood of an accident is redundancy. At least two separate anchors secure the line on either end. Further, in case one webbing breaks, two lines are taped together. As beginner and even intermediate highliners, participants wear a leash attached to a climbing harness. The leash trails behind the person, clipped securely onto the line. With experience, athletes can opt to remove the harness and tie the leash to a waist strap called a swami belt. Though less cumbersome, this makes for an uncomfortable and often painful fall. The most minimal amount of security is when the leash is tied to one ankle. This is for experts only—those who assume they will not fall. Dangling by one ankle is not life-threatening, but it could definitely lead to injury. Lastly, free soloing is when there is no leash or safety apparatus at all. Those who attempt this only do so when they have mastered the sport and are certain they could catch the webbing if they did fall—versus falling to their deaths.

Faith soon racked up hundreds of hours of experience. Now an expert, she was approached by a film company and offered a contract. They hired her for a commercial to sell Volvo trucks. The sponsor wanted to demonstrate the capability of the truck and devised a stunt that was risky, dangerous, and exhilarating. Would Faith be willing to walk along a wire between two moving trucks? Would she be able to do it before the trucks reached a split tunnel where the wire would snap as it hit the wall separating the two?

By now, Faith had earned worldwide recognition. A top athlete in the sport, she had secured several women's world records, including longest highline—317 feet (96.5 m) in length—and longest free solo, a feat where the highliner walks without a leash or any other safety harness. Here she had walked unattached for 92 feet (28 m), knowing that a fall would result in her death. Faith's other records included the farthest longline—a 728-foot (222 m) slackline rigged closer to the ground—along with the longest waterline. Over water, her nearly 460-foot (140 m) walk was especially difficult because the movement of the water disrupted her sense of balance. Compared to the Volvo stunt, Faith had walked higher and farther. However, she had never walked between two moving vehicles. This was different—and harder—than anything she had done so far.

The commercial was filmed in Vrgorac, Croatia, on a highway that was closed to regular traffic. In the 11 days of practice and filming for the stunt, Faith learned just how difficult the objective was. The trucks would need to remain exactly the same distance apart the whole way down the highway. If they veered even a couple of inches one way or the other, the wire would snap or loosen. Either way would throw Faith off. Similarly, the trucks would need to maintain precisely the same speed. Then there was the force of the air. While on the wire between the trucks, she would need to fight a wind tunnel that made it nearly impossible to stay upright. Because of these factors, the stunt crew included several expert medics and a fully equipped ambulance.

A team secured the cable to the top of each truck. The commercial shows Faith climbing up the aluminum ladder to join them. She tugs on the line, testing it to make sure it wasn't going to slip or break. Satisfied, she clips a leash on her ankle. Hovering nearby is a helicopter with a cameraman onboard. After a countdown of "one, two, three," the truck drivers accelerate, and the scene unfolds.

Though the actual commercial is an amalgamation of several days' worth of film clips, Faith did accomplish the walk between the trucks during practice. The most dangerous part, she recalls, was leaping from the wire to the top of the second truck. This was moments before the trucks entered the separate tunnels, causing the wire to snap against the cement divider.

The stunt had been fun and a real adrenaline rush, but now it was time to go back to the mountains. Traveling all over the world, the settings Faith was highlining in were stunning. Her passion for the sport increased along with her skill and mental fortitude. Intent on energizing others to experience this clarity and awareness of fear, she began accepting public speaking invitations, including a TEDx Talk. Then, in an effort to bring more recognition to the women in the sport, she organized a women's slacklining festival.

The Women's Highline Meeting (formerly called the Girls Only Slackline Festival) is held annually in the Czech Republic in a place called Ostrov. Faith chose the location for several reasons. First, it was centrally located and, with many of the women coming from European countries, this made it easy to get to—not to mention that it was only one and a half hours from the Prague airport. Second, the fixtures for the highlines were close by; access to the stone towers they were rigging their lines to was only 10 to 15 minutes away from where they were staying. Finally, Faith knew the owner of a local campsite, and he was willing to sponsor their accommodations. It was ideal.

Faith's goal for the event was to encourage women in the sport. Other coed festivals were fun, but they could be intimidating to beginners when men outnumbered the women by such a large margin. Faith explains, "The focus is on women; connecting, empowering, and being a majority." Since it's a chance to celebrate being female in the sport, participants often dress up in costumes to walk the highlines. The first time Faith tried adding high heels to her ensemble while traversing a highline was at this festival. It added a level of challenge, but she managed it with no problem.

Faith reached celebrity status in the highlining community. She was a serious contender for anyone, female *or* male. She was highlining in at least ten countries a year, including Tasmania, Brazil, China, Morocco, and all over Europe. While events still had many more male participants than female— sometimes at least a 10:1 ratio—she was helping to encourage women to try the sport. People sought her out for interviews and closely followed her world-record-breaking achievements. By now she had amped up her game in another way. Faith had decided to untie her leash and try free soloing.

When Faith walked a highline with no safety harness or leash of any kind, she described the experience as the ultimate freedom from inhibiting fear. Confident that she can grab onto the line if she ever falls, Faith loves the pureness of free soloing—there is nothing holding her back from the feeling of pure freedom. "Fear is like a muscle," she says. "If you work on it, you can gain control of it and not let it direct your life."

What's next? What now? Faith decided to set up a home base at a beautiful cabin in Moab, Utah. Never one to stand still, next she learned how to use power tools in order to renovate a 1970s vintage Airstream trailer and created a mobile home that gives her the flexibility to travel around the country. Faith also plans to continue her work empowering other women. She contributes to blogs, gives interviews, and is constantly on the lookout for the next project. She feels a supreme confidence that her thirst for beauty and freedom will continue to be a lifelong pursuit. In her down time, you can hear the lovely strains of Faith's beloved ukulele:

> *Then the mountains called my name,*
> *There I met the wind and rain*
> *I met fear like never before,*
> *But I found balance to explore.*

Whose Idea?

Though inspired by a practice that is thousands of years old, the birth of slacklining is much more recent. Originating with the rock-climbing community in Yosemite National Park in the early 1980s, slacklining is different from tightrope walking. For one, the walking surface is a narrow, stretchy band called webbing that behaves more like a trampoline than a taut rope or cable. Though stability and self-control are critical to both sports, slackliners do not use a pole to help them balance.

In 1983, two climbers attempted to walk a high wire strung 55 feet (17 m) across a nearly 2,900-foot (880-m) chasm in Yosemite Park called Lost Arrow Spire. They were unsuccessful, though thankfully not hurt. However, their efforts inspired another climber, Scott Balcom, who is credited as the first slackline walker. Using nylon webbing instead of a cable, he walked along a 30-foot (9 m) expanse set up under the State Route 134 bridge in Pasadena, California. Since then, the sport has gained worldwide popularity.

Follow Faith Dickey Online

Website: http://thatslacklinegirl.com/

Instagram: @thatslacklinegirl

Twitter: @thtslacklinegrl

Facebook: Faith Dickey

Melanie Curtis: Free Fall Freedom

Fact: The speed of free fall—that period of time before you've deployed your parachute—initially increases until air resistance kicks in. Then, the steady rate of fall is about 120 miles per hour (193 kph).

Fact: Anyone in healthy condition can skydive, although in the United States you must be at least 18 years old. In 2019, Kathryn "Kitty" Hodges was 103 years and 129 days old when she went skydiving for the first time.

Fact: Statistically, skydiving is safer than driving a car. In the millions of skydives per year in the United States only a handful of people die, mostly due to human error.

Melanie Curtis was 18 years old when she tried skydiving for the first time. She had thought about it for a while, but the decision to actually do it was quick. One day she announced, "Tomorrow I'm jumping."

The momentous day started with a mandatory jump class. The lessons were nothing new. Melanie's dad owned a small plane and ran a drop zone (a designated place where skydivers land) from the back of his house. He had taken her for her first plane ride when she was three months old. Later, when he opened the skydiving center, Melanie had spent time in the prejump class and had watched plenty of skydivers launch themselves from her dad's plane. Despite this, she wasn't sure she would ever try it herself. *Why jump out of a perfectly good airplane?* she asked herself. She added, *And risk death?* But curiosity tugged at her. She wondered what it would feel like to float down to earth. How would it be away from the sound of the plane's engine with nothing but air between her and the ground?

The safety lesson that morning took on real meaning. Now it wasn't just arbitrary facts. The information and follow-on practice were for *her*. This was all about how to do it right and not get hurt. Melanie focused on understanding the function of each piece of the parachute and how the equipment worked. She rehearsed properly exiting the airplane. She learned how to maneuver her body to keep stable in the wind. She examined her gear and practiced how she would pull the steering toggles attached to the chute to control her direction and landing. Finally, she was ready. Nervous, but ready.

Melanie would be jumping solo—there was no option at her dad's business to fly tandem (strapped to an instructor), which is how many first-timers begin. Instead, she would fly with a static line parachute. This meant that there would be a line attached to the airplane when she jumped out. Within seconds, the line would grow taut, pull off a cover, and automatically deploy the parachute strapped to her back. While the line and cover stayed with the plane, the freed chute would guide her descent back to earth.

The parachute Melanie was using would be large and forgiving, too. She was glad because she knew that the larger the chute, the slower her fall would be. That first jump was meant to be gentle and controlled. The lesson also covered what to do if there was a malfunction. If something did go wrong, her equipment included a reserve chute. She learned how to cut away the faulty main chute in an emergency and deploy the reserve.

Thankfully, Melanie's equipment worked exactly as it was supposed to. Once she cleared the plane, the static line quickly grew taut. Then the line dropped away and she felt the tug of the parachute inflating above her. The time it took to glide back to earth was life changing. It was *nothing* like being in an airplane. It was a moment of such beauty and serenity that Melanie knew she would be doing this again. When she finally landed, she felt as if her brain had just been rewired.

Melanie thought a lot about that first jump. She realized that despite her brain telling her to be afraid, or that she couldn't and shouldn't, the jump had been controlled and safe. She *was* capable. She *had* done it! Melanie learned to question whether a fear she had was truly warranted and because of a legitimate danger. If not, she learned to rethink that anxiety and go for it.

After that day, Melanie knew one thing for certain: somehow she was going to make skydiving a big part of her life.

Melanie grew up in two worlds. She was a child of divorced parents, so she spent her weekdays with her mom and stepdad. On the weekends, she went to live with her dad, a small-engine pilot whose tiny airport and drop zone were located behind his house in upstate New York. Verona Skydive Center was an exciting place. Melanie loved watching the skydivers jump from her dad's plane, free falling to earth and then deploying their parachutes so they could land behind the house. After her own first jump, she was "passionately, insanely in love with skydiving."

When Melanie graduated from high school, her parents expected her to go to college. She wanted to as well, and she poured herself into studying business and finance. Despite her dedication to school, she continued to skydive whenever she had a chance. During a semester abroad in Australia, she logged almost 100 jumps. Then she graduated, and she began a career in investment banking. She continued to crave skydiving, but it was hard to find the time.

BSR Basic Safety Requirements

Over time, improvements in equipment and procedures have made skydiving safer. The United States Parachute Association (USPA) is an organization that regulates the sport in the United States. First-time participants must attend safety training led by a USPA-approved instructor. Another huge upgrade to the sport is the Automatic Activation Device (AAD), a device that automatically opens a parachute at a predetermined time or altitude. Unless flying while connected to another, experienced jumper, all beginners must wear a helmet. Luckily, traditional round parachutes have been replaced by rectangular-shaped chutes which offer more control and easier landings. Although less regulated for expert skydivers, wind and weather conditions must be within a reasonable range for a novice to make a jump. A beginning skydiver must also deploy her parachute at a higher altitude, up to 5,500 feet (1,680 m). An average altitude for starting the jump is about 13,000 feet (4,000 m). This gives the jumper 60 seconds of free fall before she deploys her parachute.

After five years at her high-stress job, Melanie decided to move closer to a place where she could skydive more often. She moved from New York City to California. There she began coaching and mentoring other skydivers. She also began competitive skydiving. Melanie was part of a four-person team that earned a gold medal in the amateur division of the US Nationals.

Performed as a competition, formation flying requires team members to link together in the sky to create geometric patterns. Flying with others in this way involves huge amounts of coordination and practice. The sport is highly technical and requires expert ability and stamina. At an altitude of 10,500 feet (3,200 m), the four members of Melanie's team would exit an airplane along with a cameraperson responsible for filming the performance. From the moment the first person exited the plane, the team had 35 seconds to connect with each other and create a sequence of predetermined formations. For each successful formation, the team scored one point.

The video recording of each event was critical to making sure the planned pattern was done accurately. With names like donut, caterpillar, or side flake opal, these formations were daunting to create. All the members of Melanie's team needed to get into precise positions, know exactly when to grab onto their teammates and where, and time falling away from each other perfectly.

After the win at the Nationals, Melanie came to a crossroads decision: should she quit her investment banking job to focus exclusively on skydiving? The trouble was, if she wanted to be a professional skydiver, she would need to eliminate every other distraction and time commitment from her life. Sure, she was enjoying the skydiving she was doing each weekend, but she didn't have time to get better. There was so much more she knew she wanted to learn and do: how to drop headfirst, how to build other team formations in the air, and many other techniques that set pro skydivers apart from hobbyists. She hesitated . . . but was this another case of how fear could inhibit her progress? Melanie wrote down her goals. Then she gave her notice at the bank.

Now Melanie needed to figure out how to make skydiving into a career. At first, she took a job at the drop zone where she had been spending all her free time. At the new job, she helped manage the business and organize "boogies," weekend events where skydivers of all skill levels got together to skydive and have fun. The job provided Melanie with a salary, but most important, it was an opportunity to get in a lot of jumps. It was hard work. It was a dream come true.

Parachuting Pioneers

André-Jacques Garnerin was 28 years old when he jumped from a hot-air balloon in 1797. Inventor of the frameless parachute, he used an open, umbrella-shaped piece of canvas to land, shaken but safe, on the ground. Watching from below was Jeanne-Genevieve Labrossea, the woman who later became his wife and the first known female parachutist. Over a hundred years later, Georgia "Tiny" Broadwick was the first woman to parachute from an airplane. On June 21, 1913, she sat on a device her adoptive father, Charles Broadwick, had attached to the outside of the plane's cockpit. When she dropped from this seat, a line running from her folded parachute to the plane stretched and automatically opened her chute. Georgia's job was to then land safely. After she had completed many successful jumps, the military took notice. Soldiers needed a way to bail from a damaged airplane or drop into rough terrain. Happy to help, Georgia demonstrated how to use a parachute and was later made an honorary member of the 82nd Airborne Division out of Fort Bragg, North Carolina.

Melanie worked for the drop zone until she decided to take her skydiving career a step further still. She quit that job so she could participate in more demonstration jumps (exhibition skydives into public places), stunts, competitions, and commercial work. These included jumps into Dodger Stadium (wearing a bathing suit and fighting unpredictable wind), into a Girl Scouts event, and once outside a church and school in Mexico with tons of kids watching. Bringing recognition to women and to the sport she loved so much, Melanie helped break world records and stereotypes. Throughout her journey, she maintained an enthusiasm and camaraderie that, combined with a fun sense of humor, helped her build a community of friends and supporters. Whatever she was involved in, Melanie was having fun.

Being a pro skydiver meant that Melanie earned her living by doing the sport she loved. The first commercial she participated in was for Jack's Burgers, a restaurant chain located in several southern states. A representative from the company approached Melanie about doing the commercial, and she signed on immediately. Now she just had to figure out how to grab a paper bag–sized object from midair.

The commercial opens with Melanie in a small airplane, wearing her skydiving equipment but acting too afraid to jump.

When a bag containing a Jack's hamburger is staged to fly out of the airplane, Melanie dives after it. It was an exceptionally difficult stunt. The weighted bag was oscillating like crazy in free fall, and it took several attempts before she was able to grab it. The commercial ends with a shot of Melanie contentedly eating the burger. The project was further affirmation that Melanie could enjoy herself and earn a living at the same time.

How Does a Parachute Work?

A skydive consists of three main stages: free fall, parachute deployment, and landing. Modern equipment includes a main parachute and a reserve. Both are packed into a container that looks like a backpack. When it's time to deploy the chute, a pilot chute (called the drogue) releases first. When it inflates, the drogue pulls 7 to 10 feet of nylon webbing from the container. This webbing is attached to risers—straps on the container—and the parachute canopy. Most modern canopies are rectangular in shape. They have several chambers that become rigid when they inflate in the force of the wind. Once the parachute is filled with air, the skydiver can use steering toggles to manage the direction of her descent. To land, a skydiver turns into the wind and pulls both toggles to further slow herself down.

Melanie sought out other opportunities. After winning award after award, her team earned the gold medal at the USPA

Nationals for Vertical Formation Skydiving (VFS). In this sub-discipline, skydivers maneuver their bodies so they are falling headfirst toward earth. This greatly increases their velocity. Instead of free falling at about 120 miles per hour (190 kph), VFS flyers speed toward the ground at up to 180 miles per hour (290 kph). Since the increased rate makes it dangerous to deploy a chute, skydivers must switch to a horizontal position before opening their parachutes. Gaining more and more skill, Melanie honed her expertise. Then she decided to try something new.

Different Dives

Skydiving today has splintered into many different subgroups. While many people skydive purely for fun, others participate in intense competitions, including the following:

Formation skydiving: Teams typically of four, eight, or more people form specific patterns in the air by holding onto each other. They earn points for each successful formation made within a certain time limit. When teams have a large number of members, the formation skydiving is called "big way." These can include up to hundreds of coordinated skydivers.

Vertical formation skydiving (VFS): Experts amp up the challenge—and speed—of formation skydiving by creating various configurations while flying *headfirst* to the ground.

Canopy relative work (CRW) or canopy formation: This is when teams create "stacks" or layers of many parachutes connected together. Here, the canopies used have special grips so that flyers can dock—hook onto—other parachutes, forming beautiful diamond shapes in the sky.

Freestyle: This subgenre allows a skydiver to get creative. The freestylist does a range of acrobatic moves—even dance moves—in the sky while a cameraperson films nearby.

Melanie joined a group of women intent on one goal: they wanted to break the world record for the largest female VFS formation. To beat the 2010 record of 41 women, it took two years of selecting the most qualified people, and then, once the list was finalized, training vigorously both on the ground and in the air. Three airplanes were needed to transport the team of 63 women and five camera flyers. Flying to an altitude of 18,000 feet (5,490 m), the members of the team wore helmets and masks that provided them with supplemental oxygen. Once they exited the plane, they had 90 seconds to organize themselves in the air, grasping onto each other while free falling headfirst.

On December 1, 2013, at Skydive Arizona, everyone packed into the airplanes one last time. They had attempted—and failed—their mission eleven times already. Nevertheless, nobody was ready to give up. Melanie knew she had the skills to perform the feat. She knew she was with an exceptionally talented group of women. Coming from 18 countries and ranging in age from 20 to 53 years old, the team members were the best of the best. In her mid-thirties, Melanie was in top shape and had performed thousands of jumps. But after so many tries, she began to wonder if making a 63-person formation was even possible.

Seconds before the twelfth jump, the air in the plane was charged with determination and grit. Then it was time. Go! Melanie shuffled after the others out of the plane. With laser focus, she positioned her body to fly next to her partner's in the formation they had rehearsed so many times. The seconds ticked down as the inner pattern of divers flew close enough to clasp hands but not collide. Then, another circle of skydivers moved in, linking hands as well. The configuration expanded until all 63 women were connected. With seconds remaining, they organized a split-off so each person could spread out and slow down by positioning her body horizontally instead of head down. Safely distanced from each other, every woman deployed her parachute with plenty of space. Success! Melanie and the rest of the team had shattered the current world record!

Melanie's life as a skydiver has included many opportunities to contribute to the world by bringing joy to others and building relationships. She is a go-getter, an inspirational leader who does not let doubt or fear prevent her from accomplishing the goals she sets for herself. Today she is a life coach, a mentor, a businesswoman, and a published author. Her passion is skydiving, with a particular emphasis on empowering other women in a sport where, in the United States, only about 15 percent of participants are female.

Regardless of gender, Melanie loves to mentor people new to skydiving, remembering back to the days when she first thought it was irrational to "jump out of a perfectly good airplane." With more than 11,000 jumps, Melanie now feels that it is irrational *not* to. "Freedom. Community. Connection. Love."—according to Melanie, skydiving and her sky family give her these precious things in droves.

Follow Melanie Curtis Online

Website: https://melaniecurtis.com/

Instagram: @melaniecurtis11

Twitter: @11melaniecurtis

Facebook: Melanie Curtis

Part II: Extreme Ocean

Bethany Hamilton: Able and Awesome

Bethany stared at the ocean. The conditions were perfect. The sun sparkled off the water, and the waves tempted her to come and surf. It was beautiful. It could also be deadly.

Less than a month ago, on Halloween morning, the unthinkable had happened. While Bethany was idly floating on her surfboard and dangling a hand into the water, a 14-foot (4.2-m), nearly 1,400-pound (635-kg) tiger shark had attacked. In seconds, it had severed her left arm inches from her shoulder. People said Bethany had been lucky to escape with her life, and she knew that was true. Now with only one arm, she wondered how radically her life would change.

Bethany was 13 years old. Up until this point in her life, it had seemed certain that she would become a professional surfer. Since elementary school, she had been surfing competitively, collecting trophy after trophy. Recently, she had won a local "Surf into Summer" event, and shortly after that she earned second place in the open women's division of the prestigious National Scholastic Surfing Association (NSSA) championships in San Clemente, California. She already had sponsors, having earned the first one at the age of nine. But what now? What would life be like with only one arm? Would her sponsors pull their support and find someone else? Was it even possible to surf with only one arm?

It was November 26, 2003, just 26 days after the shark attack when Bethany picked up her surfboard with her right arm and stepped into the ocean. She had not been in the water since she had lost her arm. Now, with her stitches finally removed, the water called to her and she stepped into the beckoning blue.

Bethany paddled out, an odd and frustrating attempt to gain the speed she needed to slide into a wave. How was she going to paddle strongly enough with only one arm to help her? How would she push herself up on the board and then try to balance? What about all the expert techniques she had worked so hard to perfect—did they all depend on having two arms?

Bethany took a deep breath. Never mind the more advanced moves. She needed to see if it was possible to do even the basics. Prone on her surfboard, she focused on paddling one-handed into the waves. She used her feet to kick and help guide her. Once she was far enough out, the next step was to get onto her feet. But how? With one arm, it wasn't like she could grab both sides of the surfboard—the rails—and pop up like she had done hundreds, maybe thousands, of times. Instead she would have to plant her one arm in the center of the board and use it to propel her upward. She tried to get up and couldn't. She tried again.

When Bethany finally stood on her board that first time back in the water, she could feel her legs, strong and confident beneath her. They were *made* to stand on the board. Surfing *was* possible! Not the same, but doable. *I don't need easy. I just need possible*, she told herself. Now that she had figured out how to stand on her longboard, she knew that life could go on—she could still do the thing she loved most. Now she could start thinking about getting back to surfing on high-performance short boards, too. Bethany pushed away any thoughts of lurking sharks. She focused on surfing.

Many people have asked her, "Weren't you afraid to go back in the water?"

Bethany had a quick and honest answer, "My fear of losing surfing was greater than my fear of sharks."

The Truth About Shark Attacks

While there are over 500 different kinds of sharks, three species are responsible for most of the unprovoked attacks on humans: the great white shark, tiger shark, and bull shark. Despite a common misperception, the chance of a shark fatality is extremely rare. According to the International Shark Attack File (ISAF), a person is over a thousand times more likely to die in a bicycle accident than be killed by a shark.

Data aside, occasionally sharks *can* be aggressive. In order to minimize the danger, there are certain steps a person can take. First, when in the water, it is better to stay in groups since a shark is more likely to attack a lone swimmer. Since sharks can smell and taste blood in the water, do not go in the water if you have an open cut. While sharks are considered colorblind, bright colors attract them—especially yellow—because they provide a contrast to the background color of the water. The same goes for jewelry, which could be mistaken for shiny fish scales. Finally, as unlikely as it is, if you are attacked, fight back. A shark's snout, eyes, and gills are sensitive areas.

Bethany earned worldwide acclaim when, after being attacked by the shark, she decided to share her story. While it was remarkable—and horrifying—that a shark had inflicted such damage, the most incredulous part of her story is how Bethany reacted both immediately following the attack and in the days, months, and years following. Moments after the attack and with her entire limb missing up to her shoulder, Bethany was in tremendous danger as her blood colored the ocean red. Not only did Bethany need to stay calm so that an accelerated heart rate would not pump out too much blood, but also she needed to get out of the water. Fast.

A deeply religious person, Bethany prayed. She focused on helping the people she was with get her to the reef and out of the water. With her levelheaded actions that day, Bethany Hamilton shocked the world with her fortitude and resilience.

Even before October 31, 2003, Bethany did not lead a life similar to most kids. She was homeschooled, and she worked on her studies around prime surfing conditions. If she wanted to grow up to be a pro surfer—and she had made that decision when she was eight years old—she needed to practice every chance she got. Nearly every day, Bethany was in the waves off the shore of her home in Kauai, Hawai'i. Her mom, dad, and two brothers were all avid surfers too, and they recognized early on that Bethany had a natural talent for the sport. They supported her in any way they could, though it was ultimately Bethany's drive and determination that enabled her to compete at a high level.

Bethany's daily routine was far from ordinary. After checking the daily surf report, her mom would wake her up early each morning. After a quick smoothie, Bethany was ready to go. Her mother drove their old family van to pick up Bethany's best friend, Alana, who was also a talented surfer. Then they were on their way to scout out the best waves of the morning. By the time of the shark attack, when Bethany was 13, both she and Alana were frequently traveling to various competitions.

Together they dreamed of achieving long-term professional surfing careers when they grew up.

Surfing—What and How

Surfing style and equipment have come a long way since the first recorded description of the sport in 1769. Joseph Banks was the official botanist on Captain James Cook's first South Pacific voyage. The European sailors had landed on the island of Tahiti when Joseph wrote about how the indigenous peoples were using a canoe to ride the waves in an early example of surfing.

Today, most beginners start on a longboard, which is easier to control than the shorter or wider boards. After applying a special wax to the top of the board—this helps in gripping the board—a surfer lies belly-down to paddle into the waves. Novice surfers run through a series of steps: Make sure the tip of the board is up. Make sure the board is perpendicular to the wave. When ready to catch a wave, the surfer pops up into a stance with knees bent and with one foot forward, a stance called "regular" if it's the left foot in front and "goofy" if the right foot is forward. Next, it's a matter of keeping ahead of the wave's crest and riding it as far as possible. If the surfer wipes out or falls off her surfboard, a leash attached to the tail of the board will keep the board close and prevent it from hitting other surfers.

Around midmorning, it was time to go home and get some schoolwork done, followed by lunch and then, when the studying was over, an afternoon surf session. While Bethany rode the waves, her mom often videotaped her. Later, the family could go through the tapes, critiquing and analyzing Bethany's technique. Her success was a whole-family effort. And she *was* successful. After winning her first major surfing contest at age eight, her dream of going pro seemed closer than ever. She soon garnered sponsorships from companies such as Rip Curl that financed some of her expenses in return for her endorsement of their products.

As Bethany filled her bedroom with surfing trophies, she was on her way to becoming a professional surfer—maybe even a world champion one day. It was easy to pour her energy into the sport because it was all she had ever wanted to do.

The tiger shark didn't change Bethany's dream. But it did alter her life in a mind-boggling way.

When Bethany first left the hospital after the attack, Dr. Rovinsky, the physician who had treated her, shared these wise words: "The list of what Bethany will have to do differently is long; the list of what she will be unable to do is short."

All About Adapting

Many activities that people perform every day typically involve using two arms and two hands. Tying shoelaces, zipping a jacket, or even using a knife and fork are things people with the use of both arms take for granted. With only one arm, even the simplest tasks can be challenging. How do you take off a wristwatch, for example, or squirt toothpaste onto your toothbrush? For the watch, using your teeth is helpful; when brushing your teeth, starting by holding the toothbrush in your mouth makes putting the toothpaste on easier. The fact is that, for most things, there is a way to adapt the activity for only one arm. It doesn't make losing an arm any less tragic, but modifications can make the amputee more independent.

While Bethany learned to function with one arm, the love and support of neighbors and friends began to pour in. But strangers were interested in her story, too. Media outlets were calling, soon generating a national frenzy of interviews and appearances. Even before Bethany learned to surf again, everyone wanted to talk to Bethany. Hers was a real-life hero story.

A couple of weeks after the attack, one reporter asked her, "Do you think you're going to surf again?"

"I think?" Bethany looked at him. "I *know* I'm going to surf again," she said with conviction. She explained, "If I don't get back on my board, I'll be in a bad mood forever."

A few months later, after Bethany had taught herself how to surf one-handed, more and more national media outlets wanted to cover her story. It seemed unbelievable when Oprah Winfrey invited Bethany to be on her TV show. Oprah asked Bethany during the TV appearance that aired on February 3,

2004, "Did you ever, ever for one moment think you wouldn't go back in the water?"

"I think it went through my head once or twice. But once things came clear in my mind, I knew I'd be back out there."

Indeed, with dogged determination, Bethany *had* learned to surf again, figuring out how to pull up on her board and working out a new center of gravity. One thing that proved to be extremely challenging initially was being able to hang onto her board when she dove under a wave, a maneuver called "duck diving." It was a critical move because it allowed an expert surfer to position herself exactly where she wanted to be on a wave. With only one arm, it was impossible to control the board underwater. Luckily, Bethany's dad came up with the solution.

One day Tom Hamilton watched some lifeguards help a struggling swimmer. They were using a board with handles mounted on the sides so that the fatigued swimmer could easily hang on. That was it! That was the solution to Bethany's struggle! Tom designed a handle that he attached to the middle top of Bethany's board. She could grab the handle as she ducked under the waves. It worked perfectly. She could now keep hold of her board beneath the waves and maneuver it into position.

With laser focus, Bethany worked harder than ever on the sport. She drilled relentlessly, building flexibility, balance, and strength exercises into her daily routine. She practiced both out of the water and in the waves of her home beaches. In January 2004, just three months after the Halloween attack,

Bethany entered an NSSA regional event. The judges offered her a five-minute head start to paddle out to the waves. Bethany politely said no. She didn't want any advantages. One arm or two, she would compete under the same conditions as everyone else. That day, when she earned fifth place, the audience was stunned—and ecstatic!

Next, in 2005 she earned first place in the NSSA National Championships, the same contest she had entered as a two-armed surfer two years before. That time she had placed second.

For a couple of years, Bethany continued on the amateur circuit, increasing her skills and holding her own against competitors. But what about pro surfing? The level of competition at the professional level was fierce. It was one thing to surf for fun and in amateur events; it was another to be able to compete against other highly skilled experts—all with two arms.

Bethany entered several qualifying series events—contests where it was necessary to earn enough points to be allowed into pro competitions. When she did well in these events, Bethany passed another self-identified hurdle. Pro surfing was back in reach. She knew it would take a huge amount of perseverance and hard work, but none of that mattered. What was important was that a career in the pro circuit was still an option. Bethany thanked God. Then she got to work.

Incredibly, the media hype surrounding Bethany just got bigger. Soon, she was overwhelmed by people reaching out to her, both those in the media and strangers from around the world. Bethany remained humble despite the attention. She concentrated on training hard to compete, not as a disabled person, but as a regular competitor.

At the age of 17, Bethany turned pro.

Organized Surfing—Going Pro

Sponsors look for athletes who will help them advertise their products and services. In exchange for a top athlete's endorsement, the sponsor will provide free company merchandise or even money. The World Surf League (WSL) is the main organizer for professional surfing events. The WSL develops two rounds of competition. The first circuit is the World Qualifying Series (WQS), where participants attempt to earn as many points as possible so they can then move to the next circuit, the World Championship Tour (WCT). Individual surfing events are divided into rounds and heats. Each of the heats is allotted a specified period of time—usually 20 to 30 minutes. Contestants attempt to ride waves and earn marks awarded by a panel of judges. Evaluated on a scale of 1 to 10, judges score each contestant on the quality of the wave as well as on how well the surfer performed.

In addition to competitions and training, Bethany now participated in speaking gigs and charity engagements. As people came out to hear her story, Bethany inspired many of them to overcome their own obstacles. To reach out further, she wrote books to share her experience, her struggles, and her faith.

When her book *Soul Surfer: A True Story of Faith, Family, and Fighting to Get Back on the Board* was published, it became an instant bestseller. In addition to the Oprah Winfrey interview, she received so many invitations to appear on TV shows or at events that she suddenly needed a manager. She made time for these events while she continued to compete, racking up more trophies along with awards such as the ESPY Award for Best Comeback Athlete and the Teen Choice Courage Award.

One day representatives from Hollywood called her up. Would she be interested in helping produce a movie of her life? *Wow!* When Bethany said yes, the media frenzy that ensued rocketed her to even higher celebrity status.

After the movie *Soul Surfer* came out in 2011, things got busier. Bethany met her future husband and got married in 2013. A year later she participated in a scene from the movie, *Dolphin Tale 2*, a true story about a dolphin who is fitted with a prosthetic tail when its own tail is irreparably damaged.

Today, Bethany continues to inspire and influence. A mother now, she cares for her young children while managing her surfing career, helping maintain a charity organization called Friends of Bethany, writing books, and continuing to speak at various venues. Her message is always the same: "Courage doesn't mean you don't get afraid. Courage means you don't let fear stop you from trying."

Shark attack victims are rare. True heroes are even rarer.

Bethany Hamilton is both.

Follow Bethany Hamilton Online

Website: https://bethanyhamilton.com/

Instagram: @bethanyhamilton

Twitter: @bethanyhamilton

Facebook: Bethany Hamilton

Jill Heinerth:
Into the Deep Unknown

Human beings cannot survive if their core body temperature falls even a dozen degrees Fahrenheit below normal. Yet Jill Heinerth, a certified cave diver, has jumped into waters so cold that first she had to clear away chunks of ice. If she were not wearing the proper clothing and equipment, she would have died within minutes.

Cold temperatures—and the threat of death—are nothing new for Jill. One particularly cold dive for this award winner and member of the Women Divers' Hall of Fame stands out. In 2001, Jill was part of an expedition that traveled to the coldest place on earth: Antarctica. Braving 60-foot (18-m) ocean swells and treacherous winds, Jill and her team were on a 118-foot (40-m) longboat and headed toward the Ross Sea. Their mission? Jill and her teammates planned to make history. For the first time ever, humans would dive into the ice caves formed inside an enormous iceberg that resided in this hostile sea. And it wasn't just any iceberg. Their plan was to enter and explore the world's largest recorded iceberg, a massive structure of ice the size of Jamaica. First, however, they needed to figure out how not to die trying.

Jill grew up in a small community a few miles west of Toronto, Ontario, in a town then called Cooksville (now part of Mississauga). She was an excellent swimmer and loved to go hiking and caving on the nearby Bruce Trail with her family. She also enjoyed building forts and was happy to crawl into the tight spaces she created. Jill spent downtime watching the popular television series *The Undersea World of Jacques Cousteau.*

Cousteau, inventor of the Aqua-Lung, was a bold explorer of the world's oceans. Jill was fascinated by his discoveries and vowed to investigate earth's underwater mysteries herself. She got her chance when she went to college. She learned how to dive in nearby Tobermory, a location famous for its freshwater scuba diving and sunken shipwrecks. She loved it!

At first Jill did not make diving a career. Instead, she earned a degree in visual communications from York University. Soon after graduating, she opened a graphics design business, but sold it in 1991 when she realized that her heart wasn't in it. Instead, she moved to the Cayman Islands. There she focused on diving and underwater photography. Bit by bit she built up underwater caving experiences, sometimes swimming through the narrowest cracks or into the darkest underwater terrain.

Little by little Jill earned recognition in the field. She joined cave-diving expeditions all over the world until she became an expert, a person whom others turned to with particularly challenging missions into some of the world's most treacherous underwater spaces. Jill had been diving for well past a dozen years when she joined a team sponsored by National Geographic to explore the interior of B-15, the world's largest iceberg in Antarctica's Ross Sea. It was an expedition that almost cost Jill her life—twice.

There are no trees or bushes in Antarctica and no permanent residents. The only people who travel to this continent—mostly in the "warmer" summer months—are researchers, their support personnel and tourists. Summertime in Antarctica is from December to March, with days of almost all sunlight. Depending on where you are, the temperatures can range from 14 degrees Fahrenheit (–10°C) to –70 degrees Fahrenheit (–57°C) or colder. The winter months are even colder. Jill's team planned their expedition for January.

To survive in such a harsh environment, Jill planned carefully. She wore specially designed clothing such as insulated rubber boots two sizes too big (to allow her to fit in extra layers of socks) and an equally large jacket that could fit over her diving suit. Her equipment for entering the water was just as carefully thought out. Jill made sure her dry suit didn't leak. Even a tiny hole would make her base layer damp, leading to hypothermia—and death. She wore two dive hoods and a specially designed lip shield to keep her lips insulated. She opted for a "rebreather," a mechanism that allowed her to rebreathe her own air underwater, thus ensuring warmer air.

Specialized Equipment: The Rebreather

Similar to a device used by astronauts, the rebreather has several advantages for breathing in an unbreathable environment. A loop of tubing directs air into the mouthpiece. Unlike regular scuba equipment that expels this used air in the form of bubbles, a rebreather recycles the air, scrubbing the toxic carbon dioxide from it and adding small amounts of fresh oxygen. The result is an efficient system that uses less oxygen and thus allows a diver to carry less weight and stay underwater longer. Also—critical to the harsh temperatures of deep or cold dives—the system conserves heat since the same air is recycled. The air is also more humid, eliminating the dehydration that comes from breathing dry air. In cave diving, a rebreather is especially beneficial. Without a constant stream of bubbles stirring up sediment and disturbing wildlife, divers are better able to be a part of the environment around them.

When Jill and the team set off from their New Zealand starting point, they weren't sure what to expect. Even though she had experienced many cave dives, neither Jill, nor anyone else on the planet, had ever attempted a dive *inside* an iceberg. Before the actual dive into B-15, the team had been exploring the area for some time. On the day of the first dive inside, Jill went over every worst-case scenario she could think of. Topside, she played out potential dangers and possible solutions. It was a process she went through with every dive. More than once it had saved her life. Jill knew that if any one of the situations she imagined occurred, the best result would be that the team would have to call off the dive and try again another day. The worst . . . unthinkable.

When Jill finally did drop into the water with her camera, everything seemed to be going as planned. Once in the water, she and her husband Paul explored a collapsed section of the iceberg. They discovered a crack that extended well into the ice. Excellent! This would be their entry point. As the two swam through the crack, they saw that the iceberg was secured to the seabed by columns of ice. Currents had carved out sections around the ice and, amazingly, there was plenty of sea life in the area as well. They swam past sea stars, scallops, and tunicates—marine creatures with no vertebrae. Suddenly, an unusual sound reverberated through the ice. The iceberg was shifting, and the entryway they had swam through was now a different shape. It was time to head back to the surface.

Jill was eager to dive again the next day. She and Paul swam through the same crack, but in a more stable section of the iceberg. They encountered the same awe-inspiring vista, stunning blue and white ice and amazing sea life. Then there was a problem—and it wasn't one that Jill had rehearsed or even thought about before she jumped into the water. This time, there was a tremendous current inside the iceberg. Once inside, it was impossible to swim back the same way they had come.

With no choice but to go forward, Jill and Paul swam under the ice until they could find a place to surface. Unfortunately, it was out of sight of the boat. Huge masses of ice surrounded them and cut them off from the boat with the rest of the crew. How would the men on the boat know they were there? How would the boat find them? It was like they were stuck in the middle of a jumble of towering icy puzzle pieces, all blocking their ability to see where the boat was located. Would they drift alone for hours? Even with their equipment, how long could they survive in the freezing sea?

Hypothermia, the Cold Killer

Hypothermia is when the temperature of the body dips dangerously low. In the mildest stage, rapid shivering attempts to warm the body by directing heat away from the skin and inward to vital organs. If heat loss continues, frostbite can set in. Extremities such as fingers, toes, and earlobes freeze first, turning white or grayish-blue and later black when the skin dies and hardens. If the body is not warmed soon, confusion and fatigue set in along with slurred speech and a lack of coordination.

As the body continues to shed heat, the progressive cold leads to heart failure. Severe hypothermia is when the body's core temperature is less than 82 degrees Fahrenheit (28°C). To treat someone with hypothermia, it is important to get them out of the cold and to remove any wet clothing. While the person suffering from hypothermia needs to be warmed up with warm fluids (if possible) and blankets, direct heat can damage the skin or cause irregular heartbeats. In addition, it's important to avoid initially heating the arms and legs. This can force cold blood to vital internal organs, causing their temperature to continue to plummet. Needless to say, when hypothermia is not treated quickly, death soon follows.

Meanwhile, the current had dislodged the boat's anchor. Luckily, as the boat drifted with the current and moved around a corner of the iceberg, the crew onboard saw Jill's and Paul's heads bobbing on the ice-flecked surface. To everyone, it was another reminder of how terribly—and quickly—things could go wrong.

The next day's dive brought with it another different and unexpected danger. This time, there were three divers: Jill, Paul, and another crew member, Wes Skiles. Once again, the three were fortunate to escape with their lives.

This third dive was no less beautiful than the ones before. Jill helped take pictures underwater, imagining the awe and excitement others would experience when they saw the never-before-seen images. However, it wasn't long before a real, new, and unexpected problem became apparent. The current that had prevented the divers from retracing their route previously was now even more powerful. Suddenly, the current was so strong that all three divers found themselves pinned under the iceberg. There was certainly no way to swim back, but they couldn't even swim forward. With walls of slick ice surrounding them, they were stuck. It was just a matter of time before their air supply would run out.

"A really ferocious current came up," Jill reflected later. "The cave tried to keep us."

One small thing saved them. Along the inside vein of the iceberg, the ice walls were dotted with tiny holes. These burrows were home to sea creatures no bigger than a thumb. The homes turned to fingerholds as Jill and the others pulled themselves, inch by inch, along the ice wall and away from the current. Their high-tech equipment, including the rebreather technology, allowed them the extra time and air to escape, but their progress took tremendous energy. Luckily they all made it, but it had been a close call.

That evening the team discussed tides and currents and searched for a way around the current's death grip. They decided they would attempt one more dive—though it turned out to be a disappointing one due to lack of visibility and poor conditions. Then, Mother Nature forced them to stop for good. The evening after their last dive, Jill drifted into sleep. The captain, meanwhile, was in the process of moving the ship after the anchor system failed again. His shout pierced the sunny but bitterly cold evening air. Jill scrambled after the others to the deck of the ship. Once there, she gasped at what was happening.

What had previously been one giant piece of ice was soon to be no longer. Tremors and vibrations rocked the iceberg before a definitive grinding and roaring sound shattered the air. BOOM! The greatest iceberg ever recorded fractured, sending enormous but smaller chunks rolling into the sea. Jill was thankful they were all safely out of the water; she knew that if this had occurred just hours earlier when they were exploring inside the mighty iceberg, none of them would have survived.

Floating Chunks of Ice

The Southern Ocean is dotted with floating ice. The smaller pieces are called growlers (ice shards less than 6 feet long) or bergy bits (those less than 15 feet long). But other chunks of ice are massive. Sections that can be miles long form icebergs that float for years before finally melting or breaking into smaller chunks. These large icebergs develop after snow builds up and compacts, forming an ice shelf along the Antarctic coast. When a section of this ice breaks or "calves" from the ice shelf, the frozen mass drops into the ocean. Because it's made of freshwater, which is less dense than saltwater, the ice floats in the salty ocean, though most of the it—about 90 percent—is underwater.

There are two main kinds of icebergs: tabular or non-tabular. Tabular icebergs are flat plains with steep sides. Non-tabular icebergs can be dome or wedge-shaped or have other irregular shapes. The largest recorded iceberg, B-15, broke from the Ross Ice Shelf in Antarctica in March 2000. It measured approximately 183 miles long and 23 miles wide (295 km long, 37 km wide).

Jill is aware of the dangers of her chosen profession. Therefore, whenever she dives, safety is always her top priority. Many people perish every year while cave diving. For example, Wes Skiles, an expert diver and member of the Antarctic expedition, died several years later while doing a routine dive off the coast of Florida. Despite the danger, Jill feels that what she's doing is important. Like any true explorer, Jill's motivation is driven by something greater than simply her own desire to discover something new. Her research and her contributions to the scientific community have far-reaching consequences.

A recent project took Jill to the earth's opposite pole. This time she was in the Arctic, tracking the path ice takes when it sheers off from the coast of Greenland and heads to Baffin Island and then south to Newfoundland. The expedition was being financed by the Royal Canadian Geographic Society, which was interested in studying the effects of the earth's warming climate. Jill was also doing some filming for her latest documentary, *Under Thin Ice: Climate Change in the Arctic.*

Jill and the rest of the team camped on the sea ice which, in some areas, was melting far more and far quicker than it ever has in recorded history. One night was particularly slushy. The base of her tent was submerged in a couple of inches of icy water. She slept on a raised cot and had to pull all her equipment

above the tent's base as well. "I have seen a steady and fright-
ening loss of sea ice. It sets up later each year and breaks up
earlier. The ice is thinning." The impact of this phenomenon
is that it disrupts the interconnected ecosystem, from the tini-
est life-sustaining ice algae to top-of-the-food-chain predators
like the polar bear who, Jill noted, seemed skinnier than in
years past. Jill believes that because they aren't getting as much
food, the polar bears are particularly hostile.

The polar bear threat required constant vigilance during
the Arctic expedition. Members of the team were on 24/7 polar
bear watch. The creatures were constantly hunting the humans,
so revving the snow-machine engines or firing warning shots
with a gun was necessary to keep them away from the camp.
One day Mario Cyr, Jill's cohost in the documentary they were
working on, suggested Jill get up close to the animals. She
agreed to photograph the majestic animals from the water.

Apex of the Arctic

Polar bears are carnivorous—they eat meat, preferably
seals. They have an excellent ability to smell and will wait
for hours at a seal's breathing hole in the ice. When the
seal pops up from the hole, the bear is ready to grab it in
its massive paws, though they aren't always successful. A
male polar bear can weigh 800 to 1,300 or more pounds
(360–590 kg), though a female is significantly smaller.
They are called apex predators because no other animals
hunt them.

Polar bears are uniquely suited to the frigid temperatures of the Arctic. Though the bears appear to be white, their outer covering of insulating hair is actually made up of air-filled, transparent tubes. Next, they have an undercoat of fur attached to black skin. The black color absorbs heat from the sun. To further keep them warm, polar bears have a layer of fat that is two to four inches thick. While they live mostly on the ice, these bears are also excellent swimmers.

Jill and her team saw plenty of polar bears, but they needed to find the right one to photograph. They wanted to film a polar bear that was not too aggressive. In other words, they needed to find a bear they could take pictures of without having it attack. Their test was simple. The team pointed their 24-foot (7.3-m) motorized canoe toward a bear. If the bear turned and started to charge them, it was deemed too hostile. After several encounters, they finally found a bear that was relatively uninterested. This was Jill's chance. She checked her equipment and prepared to get in the water, where she would photograph the polar bear from below the surface.

When Jill jumped into the water with her high-tech camera, she made sure they were in open water. Near land or floating ice, the bear had a much better chance of grabbing onto her. There was a problem, though—her neoprene hood made her look like a seal and thus a tasty meal for a hungry polar bear. Because of this, she had a vital piece of safety equipment with her. Jill was carrying 50 pounds of lead weights in case the bear did decide to hunt her. At the first sign of trouble, Jill would dive deep and the weights would help her do that fast. She was pretty sure—but not one hundred percent certain—that the polar bear wouldn't follow her. She knew that polar bears *could* dive, but she hoped this one wouldn't want to go too deep.

While actually photographing the polar bear, Jill admits she was scared. Underwater, the bear saw her, focused right on her, and thankfully kept going. It was an incredible shot. She probably wouldn't do it again.

Today, Jill works as a water conservationist as well as an underwater archeologist. She is also an author who shares her insight and experience to groups all over the world. Her inspiration for her work stems from a goal to motivate young people. She has wise advice for others, too: "Ask for help. Ask for advice. . . . Do something that scares you. Know that anything is possible with hard work and commitment."

When she stops to ponder the consequences of her accomplishments, Jill may reflect on the words of her childhood hero, Jacques Cousteau: "From birth, man carries the weight of gravity on his shoulders. He is bolted to earth. But man has only to sink beneath the surface and he is free."

Follow Jill Heinerth Online

Website: www.intotheplanet.com

Instagram: @jillheinerth

Twitter: @jillheinerth

Facebook: Jill Heinerth

Ann Marie Stephens:
Weightless and Free

Ann Marie Stephens is an experienced scuba diver who has gone diving near blacktip sharks, grey reef sharks, nurse sharks, and even the unusual Wobbegong shark on a trip to Australia. While these sightings were amazing, none of *those* sharks were 20 feet long (6 m). None weighed up to 1,000 pounds each (450 kg). None were as imposing or awe-inspiring as the great hammerhead shark. While the International Shark File states that hammerheads do not generally attack humans—most of the time—it was a rare and thrilling treasure when Ann Marie got to see a huge school of the sharks firsthand.

Ann Marie was visiting Fiji, a country made up of more than 300 islands located in the South Pacific Ocean. She had chosen the location because of its reputation for spectacular diving and stunning scenery. So far, she had not been disappointed. Now on an early morning dive, she planned to spend as much time as she could in the water, hoping to see some interesting wildlife. This would be an open-water dive; there were no reefs or other landmarks under the surface here. It would be an immersion into the continuous, endless blue.

On the boat, water stretched to every horizon. Ann Marie did a final safety check of her scuba equipment. Her mask was clear. The air tank was full. Each strap was snug, but not too tight. She placed the regulator—the piece that would feed her air from the tank—in her mouth and confirmed that the air was turned on and that nothing was leaking. At last, stepping onto the platform at the back of the boat, she dropped into the water with the rest of the day's divers. She sank under the surface where the water was warm and peaceful, a beautiful reprieve from her everyday hectic life.

Bang! Bang! Several minutes into the dive, a metallic clang interrupted the quiet. One of the divemasters—the leaders of the group—knocked on her tank to get everyone's attention. She pointed to a grayish blur forming in the distance. A shadowy fin emerged, and then Ann Marie saw a uniquely shaped head followed by a powerful, streamlined body. The unmistakable rectangular feature made it easy to identify the enormous creature swimming nearby; it was a great hammerhead shark. In a moment, another shadow joined the first and then another. Soon, dozens of hammerheads glided effortlessly past the mesmerized divers. It was astonishing and beautiful. Ann Marie wished there was a way to make the moment last.

Beautiful and Bizarre: The Hammerhead

There are nine different species of hammerheads. The largest is the great hammerhead, which can grow up to 20 feet long (6 m), though 12 feet (3.6 m) is the average. One thing all hammerheads have in common regardless of their size is their uniquely adapted head, shaped like a rectangular, double-sided hammer. This shape allows them to maneuver quickly. Also, with eyes on either end of this flat appendage, they have a wide field of view.

Along with a keen sense of smell, another feature that helps hammerhead sharks thrive in the ocean is their ability to detect the tiny electrical impulses given off by other creatures. To locate prey, thousands of receptors under their heads pinpoint these signals so the shark can hone in. In addition, great hammerheads have triangular teeth with sharp, cutting edges. This allows them to tear through their favorite prey, the stingray, which they sometimes find hiding on the sandy ocean floor in warm waters around the world. As these teeth become worn and fall out, sharp, new teeth grow in their place.

From her earliest memories, Ann Marie has always loved the water. However, she opted out of joining her sisters on the swim team in elementary school. She never took swim lessons, either, but simply learned naturally how to stay afloat. At her family's community pool, she loved to wrap one leg around the other and pretend she was a dolphin or a mermaid.

Though she spent hours in the pool, the ocean was a mysterious and fascinating world that she admired but knew little about. That changed when she took an oceanography course in high school. The more she learned, the more she became intrigued by the incredible wildlife teeming in the ocean's depths. It hadn't yet occurred to her that she could learn to scuba dive and experience seeing these creatures firsthand.

Ann Marie had graduated from college and was working as a teacher when she went on a life-changing trip with her sister, Sara. They were snorkeling in the Great Barrier Reef off the coast of Australia. It was fun, but Ann Marie was more interested in what was happening below them; it seemed to her that a group of scuba divers were having a much better time. She spit out her snorkel. "That's what I want to do!" she told her sister.

Following through with her promise, when Ann Marie got home to Virginia, she looked up the location of the closest dive shop. Then she called them up. Yes, they gave lessons on how to scuba dive. Yes, she could start right away. The company would supply all the necessary equipment; all Ann Marie needed to do was show up. Convincing her partner, Scott, and a close friend to join her, soon Ann Marie was working toward getting her C-card, a license to scuba dive.

Scuba Certification

Earning a license to scuba dive starts with a dryland course that can now be found online. This introduction goes over the basics such as safety and equipment. The gear necessary to scuba dive includes a mask, fins, buoyancy control device (BCD), regulator, tanks, and a pressure gauge. Essential safety lessons cover how to clear water that has leaked into your mask, how to breathe from a regulator, and what to do to control buoyancy, or how fast or slow you sink. It also covers emergencies, like how to share a regulator if your own equipment malfunctions underwater. The one thing the course emphasizes over and over: never scuba dive alone. The course moves onto real-life practice, usually starting in a swimming pool and then relocating to open water. Here, beginning scuba divers stay within a depth of no more than 60 feet (18 m).

During the initial days of her training, Ann Marie practiced in the deep end of a pool. She sat on the bottom, wearing a belt with weights to hold her down and breathed from a tank of air on her back. It was the strangest feeling! She was surrounded by water, yet her lungs were filling with air. She had to remind her brain that it was OK—she had a steady air source and she didn't need to hold her breath. It was important to train herself to recognize that she was safe because the next segment of the course took things a step further. This time she wouldn't be diving in her local swimming pool.

Phase three of the course involved a real dive in deep water. The dive site was Millbrook Quarry in Virginia. Ann Marie was thrilled to take this next step, but it was a boiling hot summer day and uncomfortable to wait outside wearing her wet suit. The tanks were heavy, too. For a small-boned woman, it was challenging to haul her equipment into the water. Once submerged, though, the cold seeped into her wet suit. Now she was shivering nonstop.

Under the surface, the sound of her breathing was loud as Ann Marie inhaled through her mouth and then expelled a stream of bubbles. She adjusted for her restricted sight, too, since the sides of her mask limited her peripheral vision. She descended, playing with buoyancy until she figured out how to maintain a certain depth. It was like there was no gravity under the water. She didn't need her arms, either, but used her fins to propel herself forward. Suddenly the instructor swam into her field of vision. He checked on her by forming a circle with his thumb and first finger. *Are you OK?*

Oh yeah, Ann Marie thought. *This is exactly where I want to be.*

When the dive course ended, Ann Marie received a license to scuba dive anywhere in the world. Now it was time to plan her first trip under the ocean, the beginning of a lifetime of underwater adventure. It was only fitting that she chose the Great Barrier Reef.

Excited and determined to start this new journey, Ann Marie saved up her money until soon she and a friend were flying to Australia. The night before the dive, she organized her new gear. She didn't want to waste a minute sorting things out the next morning. Once on the boat, she looked across the choppy waves. It was raining, but that didn't matter. She was going to get wet anyway. When she stepped off the boat and sank under the water, she had an immediate sensation of calmness. She checked her equipment as water filled her ears. Her buoyancy was under control. Her mask was secure. Her regulator was providing her with plenty of air. She was weightless.

"I looked around me and fell in love. . . . Here I saw coral, bright-colored fish, and a small reef shark within my first couple of minutes. I felt so at home. Of all the places I'd been on land, nothing compared to the feeling of being submerged in the ocean."

She completed two dives that day. It wasn't enough. Even though she was new to the sport, Ann Marie felt completely comfortable. Her breathing slowed as she took in all the ocean had to offer. No phones rang. No students were calling her name or tugging at her to get her attention. There were no meetings or papers to grade. Instead, the water enfolded her into an embrace that seemed to whisper to her, "Here, let me hold all of this stuff for you while you enjoy my beauty unencumbered."

Under the Surface: Let's Talk

For safety reasons, divers need to be able to communicate underwater. To do so, they use a system of hand gestures. A looped thumb and first finger means everything's OK, but a thumbs up means it's time to go to the surface. Other gestures indicate when you're out of air—in which case a buddy will share hers until you can get out of the water—or that there's danger nearby. (There's a sign for "shark.")

Since you can't shout a warning under water, divers must attract attention another way. Often the dive master, the expert in charge, will bring along simple noisemakers such as a tank banger or a shaker. A tank banger is a hard, plastic ball attached to a band that fits over the air tank. To make a loud clang, the diver grabs the ball and lets it snap back against the metal tank. Another inexpensive option is a shaker, a small device that makes a loud rattling sound.

It's not all about danger, though. To ask a question or share something they've found, some divers bring along a small plastic slate with a wax pencil for writing on it. There are high-tech devices, too. However, since they are expensive, most recreational divers go with the simpler options.

To commemorate the experience of her first dive, Ann Marie bought a special strap for her mask. She vowed that when she took her next trips, the strap would go with her, a memento of that first magical dive. It didn't take long to discover new diving destinations, either. Sometimes Ann Marie was inspired by reading something on the Internet or by noticing a picture on a poster or calendar. She also pored over diving magazines to find the best scuba diving sites in the world. Each location offered more thrills. There was unbelievable beauty and a diversity of creatures so mind-boggling that it spurred Ann Marie to share her experiences with her students.

One day she told her class about the time she was diving off Rangiroa, an island in French Polynesia. They had spotted some grey reef sharks, 6-foot-long (2 m) creatures that generally will leave humans alone—unless they're feeding or feel threatened. Ann Marie lost sight of the creatures when, suddenly, she heard something. A high-pitched whistle resonated through the water. . . . Could it be?

Ann Marie looked around. She heard the whistle again. Suddenly, a pod of dolphins came into view. They were *huge*—and fast. They flew around the divers in a tight circle for several minutes. As Ann Marie made eye contact, she could feel their quiet intelligence. Were they there just to say hello? Were they simply as curious about her as she was about them? Or, were they somehow protecting her from an unknown threat, maybe the sharks? Whatever their reason, they stayed for a breathtaking several minutes before scooting off.

Dolphins to the Rescue

Besides being warm-blooded animals, dolphins have a lot in common with humans. For one thing, they're super smart. They communicate with each other using noises such as whistles, clicks, squeaks, and barks. They also like to hang out together, traveling in a group called a pod.

Dolphins are known to be playful, but they can also save lives. In case after case, dolphins have intervened when people have found themselves in very real trouble. In one example, a surfer named Todd Endris was enjoying the water when a great white shark attacked. At first, the shark plowed into him, sending him several feet in the air. Then the shark bit him and his surfboard. Next it grabbed his leg. That's when the dolphins came to the rescue. As Todd and witnesses describe it, the dolphins began energetically jumping over and around Todd to form a wall between him and the shark. Thanks to the dolphins, he was able to get away, ultimately surviving the attack.

The ocean has given Ann Marie treasure after treasure. Once she was on a dive in Bermuda when a moon jelly, a translucent, bell-shaped jellyfish, floated near. At about 15 feet (4.6 m) below the surface, she was doing a mandatory safety stop before exiting the ocean. This procedure helps release a build-up of nitrogen, a side effect of breathing compressed air. If Ann Marie didn't get rid of the gas by slowly expelling it from her lungs, the nitrogen could form dangerous bubbles that would cause decompression sickness—also called the bends. Though she had never experienced it, Ann Marie took the threat seriously. The moon jelly was a welcome visitor as she was going through this several minute pause.

The pulsing, translucent orb reminded Ann Marie of an opal. She watched the fascinating creature until it was time to rise to the surface. As she kicked her fins toward the boat's ladder, Ann Marie encountered another gift. This time, the entire surface of the ocean was dotted with moon jellies. They parted as she emerged from the water, making a path for her to exit. She didn't want to leave.

Ann Marie has been followed by turtles, an eel, sharks, and remora fish. She has penetrated schools of fish and watched— and often recorded on her underwater camera—stingrays and dozens of other creatures. Once a curious octopus wrapped its tentacles around her arm and over her mask. Every experience was thrilling, but there have also been reminders of how dangerous the sport can be if you don't take precautions or if you forget that you're merely a visitor in an unpredictable undersea world. She has had equipment malfunctions such as leaking hoses, ripping mouthpieces, and broken fins. In Bermuda she once had to exit the water in enormous swells because a storm had moved in while the group was underwater. It took every ounce of her strength to swim to the boat and get onboard. Another time she got swept up in currents so strong, her body was tossed around like she was on an amusement park ride. Swimming against it was exhausting—and impossible. Finally, she and her dive buddies deployed a "safety sausage," an inflatable tube that made it easier for the boat to find where they had ended up.

Wherever she is, Ann Marie has a profound respect for the ocean. She appreciates its astounding beauty, but she understands that it is still a wilderness that can be dangerous if you aren't paying attention. It also makes her sad when she sees a lot of plastic and other trash at dive sites. There are still places that provide pristine diving conditions—clean ocean, a healthy reef, and plenty of wildlife—but she says that the conditions in the ocean are declining. Pollution is a real issue.

Ann Marie has never been a professional diver. Instead, she works at her day job, teaching first grade, and follows a passion to write books, often about her experiences underwater. Diving, she admits, is an expensive hobby, especially if you're traveling all over the world to do it. Her advice about that? "Just do it. Don't wait until you have the time or money. Find a way to make the money and the time." She explains how she saves enough money for her trips. She rarely eats out. She's careful how she spends her money, and even picks up odd jobs sometimes in order to pay for the next dive.

"When you're on your way to your dream, obstacles will get in your way. When they do, leap over them, go around them, distract them, or dive right through them. *No* is not an option when you want something bad enough."

To Ann Marie, that means escaping to the enchanting world beneath the waves.

Follow Ann Marie Stephens Online

Instagram: @amstephens_

Twitter: @AMStephens_

Facebook: Ann Marie Stephens

Part III: Radical Rides

Sneha Sharma: Behind the Wheel

Sneha Sharma slid into the cockpit of car #9, her bright purple Formula 4 racer. She strapped on the 17-pound (8-kg) harness and adjusted her helmet. The temperature outside was close to 140 degrees Fahrenheit (60°C), but in the confined space of the cockpit and wearing her fire-resistant suit, it felt even hotter. She maneuvered her car into position and joined the lineup. The drivers had just finished the green flag lap, a practice round to warm up their tires and make sure that everything was running like it was supposed to.

The red lights blinked on, and two columns of drivers revved their engines. This was the moment when Sneha tuned out everything around her—the other racers, the crowds, even the mechanics. She concentrated on the vehicle surrounding her, knowing that in a fraction of a second she would be pushing it—and herself—to the limit.

Go! Sneha dropped the clutch into gear and she was off. At first it was tight. Cars jockeyed into position, pressing left and right and fighting for an opening. In the 25-minute race, each driver would make several laps while negotiating the many tight turns of the track. Earning points for how well they placed in each race, the person with the most points by the end of the championship would stand on the victory platform. Sneha hoped it would be her.

The cars were still clumped together, each driver looking for an opportunity to overtake the others. Suddenly, Sneha felt a tug on the rear of her car. Pulled out of her intense concentration on maneuvering forward, she gripped the steering column while she fought for control. The driver behind her had clipped the back of her car! Now her rear wing—the structure on the back of her lightweight vehicle that helped anchor it to the ground—was bent.

With the wing off-kilter, it was uncertain whether Sneha could keep going. It was definitely a huge disadvantage, and she wasn't going to place for this race. But more than anything, Sneha didn't want a DNF—a "Did not finish." She assessed her car's performance, listening to each nuance and feeling the altered performance. She would keep going to avoid the DNF. It was a setback, but, as she knew very well, just part of Formula racing.

Sneha grew up in Mumbai, India. As a child she loved music, dance, being by the sea—and speed. While many of the other girls had fancy pink bikes with glitter handlebars and seats, Sneha preferred a sports bike with gears. This enabled her to go fast. Often the neighborhood boys would try to race her. To their surprise—but not Sneha's—she often won. At the age of 14, Sneha tapped further into her craving for speed when she tried karting for the first time. She loved the wind flying past her and the ability to conquer the track. When she clocked the fastest time at the Hakone Go-Karting Track her first day there, she ignited a new passion that would change the course of her life.

Sneha kept coming back to the karting circuit. Her traditionally minded family, though loving, did not initially support this new hobby. This type of sport was *not* for girls. Sneha was to focus all of her energies on her studies so that she could go to college and earn a respectable degree. Karting was a distraction.

But Sneha couldn't quell her thirst for racing. With schoolwork in hand, she would pick up her helmet hidden outside, jump the wall surrounding her family's home, and head to the track. She saved her lunch money and raided her tiny savings for every rupee she could spare to practice as much as possible while still being diligent with her studies. In between sessions at the track, she opened her books and made sure she kept up with what was going on at school.

One day Sneha was at the track when she noticed two drivers going incredibly fast. She recalls, "They were driving in sync as if they were music itself." She asked the mechanics who they were and learned that they were national race car drivers. As she continued to watch, Sneha formed a kernel of resolve. This was what *she* was going to do. No matter the hurdles, Sneha vowed that she, too, would someday be a national race car driver.

The first step was to enter some local races, but how? Sneha listed the challenges she would have to overcome:

Time: She would need to find a balance between her college-bound coursework and racing.

Health: She had to get in better shape, building up her core strength, along with neck, arm, and leg muscles.

Parents: They were taking out loans to help Sneha complete her schooling and go to college. Convincing them that she could do both school and racing was going to be tough.

Finances: Racing was expensive. Until she proved good enough to secure sponsorships, Sneha was going to have to pay for this on her own.

Even her gender was an obstacle. In both bicycling and in karting, Sneha had experienced situations where boys didn't like losing to a girl. Several times, the boys she won against had spewed nastiness toward her when they lost. They didn't react the same way when they lost to another boy. Sneha steeled herself to ignore their comments and concentrate on the things she could control. When she put on her helmet, she was going to drive the best she could, and it didn't matter if she was a male or a female.

Women in Formula 1 Racing

The first woman to participate in Formula 1 racing was Italian-born Maria Teresa de Filippis. Her career began with a bet. At the age of 22, her brothers challenged her to drive faster than they could. She did—and loved it. Soon, Maria entered a number of local races. Driving a secondhand Maserati, she qualified in 1958 for the World Championship Grand Prix in Belgium. She became the first woman to race in a Formula 1 contest. Few women followed her, but on April 7, 1980, Desiree Wilson from South Africa became the first woman to win an F1 race.

Today there is still an underwhelming number of females in F1. In an effort to engage more women in this top tier of motorsport, the W Series was launched in October 2018. This all-female motorsport championship is the first of its kind. Their mission proclaims, "We're here to shake up the industry, push past stereotypes and change the face of motorsport, quite literally."

Challenges are the best catalyst to success, Sneha told herself. Unwilling to let the long list of obstacles deter her, Sneha approached the mechanics on the track where she was practicing. Would they be willing to teach her the skills necessary to race, things like how to corner or accelerate, when to brake, and the strategy for overtaking other cars? In return, she would work at anything they needed her for. They agreed and Sneha now balanced her studies and racing with jobs at the track. She learned to tune cars, managed accounts, worked with teams, and even helped load vehicles into trucks after a race. In return, she earned enough money to enter local races after obtaining her racing license. She was 16 years old.

Sneha still didn't have enough money for high-end—or even low-end—equipment. Instead of specialized clothing, she wore regular tennis shoes and soccer gloves, often developing painful blisters that she would have to tape up. Since karts are so low to the ground, Sneha felt every bump as she drove incredibly fast. Each race meant more bruises. There were times, too, when Sneha ended races with more than just discolored skin.

Once Sneha was in a tournament when she noticed that the fuel tank between her thighs was leaking. She didn't have a specialized racing suit or expensive protective clothing so there was nothing to shield her from the spill. She had a choice: quit, or ignore the pain and keep going. She couldn't, or wouldn't, let the leaking fuel stop her, despite the fact that it burned off a layer of her skin. She endured the pain for the three days of the event. "I felt like I was on fire," she recalled afterward.

Another time Sneha was racing when a kart in front of her crashed into the barrier. A chunk of the wooden curb detached and flew onto the track. Too late to swerve or brake, Sneha ran over the debris, suffering a fractured rib as she slammed into the steering column (She had not been able to afford an expensive rib protector). She went home that night, holding her arm over her aching ribs and pretending she wasn't hurt.

If her family knew she'd injured herself, she reasoned, they would try to make her stop. Bruised, battered, and now with aching cracked ribs, she went to bed only to wake up a short while later. Her family was standing around her bed, their faces looking as pained as she was feeling. It was clear to everyone, however, that Sneha had no intention of quitting.

A high-end Formula race car is built with a custom seat. While the driver sits with a plastic bag around her, a substance is poured in that will mold to her body. This custom seat helps enormously for tight left and right turns. The less the driver moves in the seat, the more control she has. Sneha didn't have this kind of seat in her kart. If she had, perhaps it would have prevented the next injury she sustained a short while later.

Sneha was doing well when a driver ahead of her crashed. Unable to avoid him, the impact of the collision caused Sneha's head to whiplash. Blacking out momentary, she gained consciousness as the safety car sped onto the scene. She was OK, but it was a reminder of how quickly things could go terribly wrong. She learned from the experience, vowing to always keep safety in mind as she pursued her dream.

Sneha participated in more and more races, building up skill and experience, as well as several podium finishes. Soon, though, she would have to put it all on hold. It was time to focus on college. There was no choice—her family needed her to earn money and to do so, she had to pursue professional training. This time, Sneha looked into the sky. Tapping into her passion for speed, she decided to become a pilot.

To train for her commercial license, Sneha spent 11 months in the United States. Taking out loans, she flew to California when she was 17 years old. It was exciting, but scary, too. What was the United States like? Would she ever be able to race again? What demands would her new profession require?

The United States was strange and different. Despite the cultural obstacles and hardships of missing home, Sneha was the first trainee in her group to fly solo. Soon, after a rigorous course in California and briefly in Miami, Sneha earned a commercial pilot's license. Ecstatic, she returned to India where she soon joined the highly competitive job market. She secured a job with Indigo Air and worked on her certification to become a pilot. It was a great opportunity, but somehow she'd have to fit in racing, too.

Whenever she had time off, Sneha went to the racetrack. She moved from kart racing to closed-top cars, which had better chances for sponsorships. With heavy student loans to pay back and a family that needed her support, money was still a very real issue. But expensive or not, Sneha was not about to give up racing. She entered competitions such as the Volkswagen Polo Cup and the Toyota Etios series. When she ranked fifth in the Mercedes Driver Development Hunt, she earned the moniker "India's Fastest Female."

All About Speed

Open-wheeled and containing a single seat, Formula race cars are made for speed, with their performance on the track measured down to thousandths of a second. The highest pinnacle of the sport is Formula 1, where drivers race over 200 miles per hour (390 kph) around a multi-turn circuit. Under this premier racing class are Formula 2, 3, and 4 racing divisions. While Formula 1 cars cost millions of dollars to custom build, Formula 4 (F4) cars are much more affordable. This is where younger drivers launch their careers.

All Formula cars have a "monocoque" body. French for "single shell," the word refers to how the car is made from a single carbon-based material, allowing it to withstand tremendous pressure. Drivers are strapped into a seat in the padded cockpit and get ready to drive up to 900 horsepower engines (160 horsepower in an F4 car), which is many times the force of a typical American car—about 120 horsepower. Because of the terrific speed generated by these engines, front and rear wings help ground the car. This downforce is especially necessary for cornering—accelerating around a curve—where the potential for the car to lift off the track is greatest. Because of their aerodynamic construction, most F1 cars can accelerate to 60 miles per hour (95 kph) in approximately 2 seconds or less.

Life was hectic. Between racing and maintaining her day job, finding enough time for everything was difficult. With little sleep, Sneha was managing working and racing, but the lifestyle was taking a toll on her body. In addition, every time she flew a plane—sometimes up to four takeoffs and landings a day—the force of accelerating and decelerating would stress her body. While she should have been taking the requisite time to recover, she was exposing her body to more pressure—g-forces—when she was on the racetrack. The strain was adding up.

G-Force Sky and Track

Gravitational force—g-force—is the measurement of pressure we feel when doing things like taking off in an airplane, riding a roller coaster, or banking around a curve in a race car. Rapid acceleration causes increased g-force or stress on the body. The more g-force you experience, the heavier things feel. What is 100 pounds (45 kg) when standing still on earth will feel like 200 pounds (90 kg) when the g-force is doubled.

A commercial airline pulls a little over one g during takeoff. A driver in a Formula 1 car can experience significantly more: five gs when braking and up to six gs when cornering. One of the most extreme examples of g-force occurs in the cockpit of a fighter jet. This exposure can cause serious problems to the pilot. Higher g-forces can prevent the heart from properly pumping blood into the brain, potentially resulting in loss of consciousness and even death.

Sneha didn't have days to rest between her duties as an airline pilot. In order to progress in her sport—by now she was driving Formula cars—she needed to train as much as possible. One day everything came crashing to a painful halt.

Sneha felt drained. In order to build strength, she had hired a yoga instructor. He pushed her farther than her body could take. Sneha ignored the pain—until she couldn't. She ended up damaging both knees so badly that it took nearly a year to fully recover. It was devastating. It was demoralizing. A highly independent person, Sneha couldn't fathom not being in complete control of her own body. Then, something worse happened: Sneha's beautiful mother passed away.

The loss of her mother reinforced to Sneha that time is precious. *Life*, she told herself, *is not run by the currency of money, but by the currency of time*. She knew that with her limited time, she needed to do what made her happy. Sitting in a race car, gearing up to speed—those were the things that made her feel truly alive. Sneha realized that guilt had been holding her back. Her performance had suffered because she had felt uncomfortable for wanting this so much.

With new resolve—and a repaired body—Sneha decided to honor her mother and her family by doing the very best she could at something she loved. That meant racing Formula cars. Sneha's job as a pilot paid a decent wage, and by now she had paid off much of her student loans and could afford to put some of her money into racing.

With success on the racetrack, life got more hectic. Sneha was now traveling internationally to participate in races, to places such as Malaysia, Austria, Thailand, and Qatar, as well as all over India. With her passion again taking an enormous amount of her time, Sneha worked out a plan with her employer. She ratcheted up her racing career by cutting her Indigo Air hours to part time.

In the Sky and on the Ground

While both involve tremendous speed, perhaps the most obvious difference between racing and flying is the purpose of each. When a pilot is flying an Airbus A320, her job is to keep the plane functioning safely. With up to 180 passengers, not including crew members, a pilot must constantly monitor that every system is not overburdened and is functioning well within its capability.

Racing is the complete opposite. Here, winners take home the trophy when they max out their machines, pushing them to the limit of what they can do. In Formula 1 racing, for instance, engines often last less than 12 races before they have to be replaced or rebuilt. Tires have even less longevity. Because worn tires slow a car down, in high-stakes races crews replace tires up to a dozen times per race, usually during every pit stop.

Today Sneha is encouraged that, while the number of women in Formula racing remains small, this statistic is improving. In 2019, when Sneha was invited to attend the qualifiers for the W Series, it was empowering to connect with so many women who are as enthusiastic about the sport as Sneha is. As she continues to compete internationally, Sneha provides serious competition for all drivers, male or female. Her technical skills are improving, and she is more comfortable behind the wheel than she has ever been. Her goal for the future? Sneha plans to be the best Formula driver she can be. "It's pure passion," she said, "because I want to drive. I got to this point because I wanted to do it for myself."

Sneha lives her life in high gear. With her foot on the accelerator, she will not be slowing down any time soon.

Follow Sneha Sharma Online

Instagram: @snehasharma52

Twitter: @snehasharma90

Facebook: Sneha Sharma Racing

Elladee Brown:
Stoked and Dialed

"Our goal is to save lives." In the wild, mountainous terrain of Canada's westernmost province, the British Columbia Search and Rescue missions—done mostly by volunteers—can be grueling, even life-threatening. When Elladee set off on a mountain-bike trip with a friend, she never dreamed that they would need to be rescued by helicopter. She had done everything right:

* *Leave a detailed trip plan.* Elladee described her route to her wife, Kara. Elladee and her friend Bjorn would start from outside Vancouver and ride to Squamish, a distance of approximately 60 miles (100 km). It was supposed to take a day.

* *Make sure you're physically and mentally ready.* An avid mountain biker who at one time ranked second in the world, Elladee definitely was.

* Take all the essential gear. This was not the first time Elladee had gone into the deep woods to travel by mountain bike. Her equipment was top of the line. She and Bjorn were using e-bike systems that fit onto their bikes (battery-powered motors that augmented their human pedaling). She had included a secondary battery in her backpack along with basic tools for fixing a broken chain, a flat tire, or other minor mechanical issues. She had also packed an air horn and bear spray to scare off grizzly bears.

Elladee and Bjorn began the trip at 6:00 in the morning at a place called Robert's Creek, located on the Sunshine Coast. It was a great day for mountain biking, not too hot and not raining. At first, they made good time. There was a trail, a series of old roads built by logging companies. The conditions soon changed. The roads weren't connected—or maintained—and with constant deadfalls and thick brush, it became less about riding along a trail and more about bushwhacking through the coastal rain forest. Several times Elladee and Bjorn had to dismount and carry their bikes. Still, according to Bjorn's GPS, they would be in Squamish by 7:00 or 8:00 that night.

The trail didn't get any easier. Instead of clearing out, it became even more unmanageable. Sections they had expected to take an hour were taking five or six. Evening came, and they were nowhere near their destination. Since it was supposed to be a one-day trip, neither had brought gear for spending the night in the woods. Fortunately, they stumbled into an empty logging camp where the caretaker, Don, let them stay in a small trailer. As Elladee drifted off to sleep, she told herself, *Tomorrow the trails will clear up.* If they could just get to Pakosha Pass . . .

Elladee's optimism proved to be wishful thinking. The next day they ran out of food while making little headway, and worse, Bjorn got hurt. He was hiking his bike through a rock scree—an area of loose rock fragments—when he slipped. He didn't know it at the time, but he had fractured his shin. There was another issue, too: this area was known for its grizzly bears. Elladee had her air horn to warn off bears, but it ran out of air that evening. For safety, she began yelling at regular intervals to alert any bears in the vicinity.

"Halllooo?" an answering call broke the stillness.

Two old-timers were out camping for the week. They brought Elladee and Bjorn to their camp, gave them food, and shared their gear. "You should hike out with us," one of the campers suggested the next morning.

Bjorn shook his head.

"But your leg . . ." Elladee tried to argue.

"No, let's just do it." If they could make it to Pakosha Pass, the other side was all downhill. "We'll be in Squamish by this afternoon," Bjorn assured her.

The two set off. And at first it seemed like everything was going to be OK. Soon, however, the overgrown terrain nearly defeated them. *This is heinous for biking*, Elladee thought. How long would it be before they ran out of food again? Or water? They had gotten lucky the last two nights, but now they weren't likely to come across another abandoned logging camp or more friendly campers.

By late afternoon, Elladee knew they were in serious trouble. They were still in major grizzly bear country. They had no food or water left. Bjorn's leg had swollen, and it was getting worse. To top it all off, Elladee had accidentally drenched herself with bear spray. The lid had knocked off the container and it had sprayed the whole side of her body, burning like anything.

One foot in front of the other, she told herself. *Just keep going.*

The helicopter came over the ridge like an apparition. Elladee's wife had been able to relay their location to the search and rescue team because of the GPS device Bjorn was carrying with him. It hadn't allowed either of them to call out, but it did include a locator for their whereabouts. It may have saved their lives.

Elladee never forgot that backwoods trip and the lesson she learned: never rely on things to go as planned and always be prepared for the worst case. She still loves the outdoors, a passion that has carried over since childhood, but she knows she must respect it and never take anything for granted.

Growing up in a tiny town in the heart of the province, Elladee describes her childhood as idyllic. Nakusp, located on the Upper Arrow Lake and part of the Columbia River system, is home to about 1,600 people, a statistic that has not changed in decades. Elladee spent most of her time there outside. She hadn't yet narrowed her focus to mountain biking but spent her time fishing, riding bikes, skiing, motorbiking (until she broke her femur when, aged nine, she had a head-on crash with a tractor), waterskiing, and other outdoor activities. Her dad built her a half-pipe ramp for her skateboard. When her brother enrolled in baseball and hockey, Elladee signed up, too.

It was an active time, perfect in so many ways. Then she moved to Whistler, British Columbia, when her parents got divorced. Shortly after the move, Elladee started riding her mom's mountain bike. It gave her freedom while offering the physical challenge that she craved. Her first real mountain bike ride was with a couple of family friends. Jen and Tom invited Elladee to ride a trail near Whistler to a place called Cheakamus Lake. It was intense! The ride, about 9 miles (15 km), was exhausting, but exhilarating, too. Hooked, Elladee began riding more and more. Then, one day when her mom gave her a newspaper clipping for a local mountain bike race, Elladee decided to enter it. The decision changed everything.

Suddenly, racing became Elladee's passion. Although she came in absolute last in that first race, the experience fueled her desire to seek other opportunities. Every time she competed in a local race, her technical skills and speed improved. Not only that, she also made a conscious effort to strengthen her body. She stuck to a special diet. She started running and going to the gym. She got up at 6:00 AM each day so she could do a regimen of stretching for an hour. She taped pictures of her favorite mountain bike racers to the inside of her locker at school.

Mountain Bike Lingo

Like any sport, mountain biking comes with its own specialized terms. Here are a gnarly few.

Bail: to crash by leaping from the bike (to avoid a worse pile-up)

Bonk: drained of energy

Dab: taking your foot off the pedal to touch the ground and prevent a crash or slide-out

Dialed in: when everything is working smoothly

Gnar/gnarl: a particularly difficult section of trail

Pump: a technique to build speed without using the pedals

Roost: the dirt that gets kicked up behind a biker on a trail

Shred: to ride in excellent trail conditions

Elladee's laser concentration paid off; she was now in peak condition. And the next race she entered changed the course of her life.

The CanAm Challenge took place in the August before Elladee's senior year of high school. The dozen or so competitors in the women's race were from California, Colorado, and across Canada. The route was along a service road that snaked from the top to the base of Blackcomb Mountain. The air was hot and dry in the village below the mountain, but much cooler on top at the starting gate.

Suddenly, it was Elladee's turn. She flew down the trail, focused on nothing but her bike and the next obstacle in her path. At the bottom of the course, she took off her helmet and wiped the grit from her face as she waited to find out how well she had done. *They must have made a mistake*, she thought as her time was announced.

No, there was no mistake. Elladee had beat everyone in the race, including the pros. Tom Hillard, from the Specialized Bike company in California, approached her. "Would you be interested in joining the Specialized team next year?" he asked. Elladee didn't have to think twice. She had one more year of high school to get through, but the day after she graduated from Pemberton High School, she drove to Durango, Colorado.

Have Mountain, Will Bike

While the first bicycles appeared in the 1800s, the idea of a bike specifically designed for off-road riding is much more recent. Mountain bikes evolved from adjustments made to regular street bikes. In the early 1970s, a group of riders from Marin County, California, decided to modify their bikes to better travel down the rough trail of nearby Mount Tamalpais (Mt. Tam). They called these customized bikes "clunkers." Soon, one of these early off-road bikers, Charlie Kelly, envisioned hosting a series of races. The "Repack Races" were born, so named because the brakes on their bikes would overheat and need to be disassembled and repacked with fresh grease after every race.

Equipment innovation followed as the races became more widely known. In 1977 another of the Tam racers, Joe Breeze, custom built 10 purpose-specific mountain bikes. However, it took several years for commercial companies to catch on. Finally, in 1982 two companies—Specialized and Univega—offered mass-produced mountain bikes for the general public. Today, mountain bikes have features such as ultra-light frames, precision gears, highly responsive brakes, and suspension systems to absorb shock.

Suddenly, unbelievably, Elladee had a professional contract. She initially qualified as an expert, the level immediately below pro, but the people she was training with were some of the people whose photos she had taped inside her high school locker! It was exhilarating; the training schedule was brutal but incredible. Along with a grueling timetable of nasty climbs in her smallest gear and the steepest downgrades—Elladee loved it—she was part of a program that included a massage therapist, a manager, flights all over the world, and a paycheck. There were heart-rate monitors, nutrition supplements, and a very structured training regimen. It was a whole new level of fitness.

At first Elladee trained for both cross-country and downhill competition before switching to just downhill. Whenever she raced, she didn't focus on winning. Instead, she told herself to live for the moment and simply do her best. Despite the expert coaching she was receiving, Elladee knew that the best advice came from within. It didn't matter how a competitor looked; racing was about much more than being in top physical shape. The contests were as much—if not more—about mental fortitude.

Mountain Biking: What Kind?

As the sport of mountain biking exploded, it developed various branches. Each subgenre has a different focus and specific bikes and equipment that are made for optimal performance. In cross-country, endurance and control are essential, as riders handle a variety of terrain including climbing and descending. Cross-country routes may include sections of gravel and mud along with banked turns and curving paths. In 1996, this genre became the only mountain bike event in the Olympics.

Next is downhill. In this form of the sport, speed, skill, and balance are key to performance. Riders walk or take a lift or vehicle to the top of the course. Then, it is all about getting down as fast as possible through a marked course. Because of the extreme speed and potential for crashing, downhill racers wear full-face helmets and other protective gear.

Another subgenre requiring full safety gear is all-mountain or enduro. Here, the focus is on navigating obstacles such as drops, jumps, and steep climbs—speed still counts, as the accumulated downhill portions are timed.

Last is freeride, a specialty where riders focus on style, adventure, and choosing the best path as they use tricks and creativity to navigate natural and manmade obstacles.

Founded in 1900, the Union Cycliste Internationale (UCI) is a global-based organization that governs all forms of cycling. Ninety years later, UCI held its first official Mountain Bike World Championships. Elladee entered the premier event along with competitors from all over the world, including Bangladesh, Botswana, Nepal, West Germany, Britain, and France. It was going to be a fierce—and dangerous—race.

The downhill competition was on a Saturday, on a day that was dry but cold in the desertlike environment of Durango's Purgatory Ski Resort. At an elevation of 10,400 feet (3,170 m), Elladee's skin felt lizardy as she warmed up with equipment from Specialized Bikes, gear that was the best of the best. In the qualifying race a couple of days before, Elladee had placed in the top five. Now, in the official event, she knew she had a chance to win, but she couldn't let that distract her. She later recalled, "You're in there and you're doing it. It's like falling asleep. You can't force yourself to do it. You just try, and it happens."

On the chairlift up to the starting gate, Elladee thought about the terrain she would be racing down. She had been allowed to try it a week ago, and she had also hiked it, analyzing the challenges and envisioning how to handle each one. Starting with a single track, the course soon split into a double track that included rocks, loose corners, berms, and a water bar that you'd have to jump or pull up on. All of that was fantastic. Elladee loved the technical stuff—it was the high speed that was scary.

For the race, Elladee would ride after Cindy Devine, a fellow Canadian and perhaps her stiffest competition. As she always did, Elladee gave herself a prerace pep talk. Instead of focusing on winning, she told herself, *This is my race, for me. Don't worry about the competitor.* She made sure everything was right: glasses on securely, tires fully functional, body and bike dialed.

Go! Elladee flew down the slope. Hurdling through every curve, jumping every obstacle, and maintaining a breakneck speed, she ultimately finished the race just 0.37 seconds later than Cindy. Elladee's performance that day elevated her to an astonishing status—she now ranked second in the world in women's downhill mountain biking!

Now and Then: Women's Downhill

As long as there have been bicycles, there have been women to race them. However, in the early history of bike racing, it was mostly a man's world, with few women taking up the sport. The same was true of mountain biking. At the birth of mountain biking in Marin County, California, Wende Cragg was frequently the sole female rider. She rode a 54-pound (24-kg) generic bike that had been modified to ride downhill.

Today, women's groups organize rides, classes, and female-centric events. Top bike companies cater to women's interest in mountain biking by building mountain bikes specifically designed for females. World class events host both male and female events where a difference of seconds determines the winners. In the 2019 UCI World Championships for downhill, for example, Myriam Nicole took first place by riding 1.204 seconds faster than her competitor, Tahnee Seagrave.

Life sped up for Elladee. As an elite athlete, her racing circuit took her all over North America, to Australia, and through nations across Europe such as Germany, Italy, Switzerland, and France. Her career racked up an impressive portfolio of statistics. All the while she continued learning. For example, in her first races she used to start off quickly. With experience she learned to pace herself, to strategize instead of going into races blindly seeking to gain speed.

Finally, a day came when Elladee was ready to step back. She found herself caring less about the rigidity of racing and more about the simple joy of the sport. She didn't feel a hunger to win, only to ride and share what she'd learned with others. It was time to do something else—still mountain-bike related, but not racing.

Elladee joined the newly evolving Women's Freeride Movement (WFM), an effort aimed at bringing the sport to more women. She participated in movies, earned her coaching certification, and began writing a regular column for a biking magazine. Why not share stories and information that would inspire others to take up the sport?

Now working as a mountain bike and accessories sales rep, Elladee advocated for adventure travel, particularly for other women. She began a series of worldwide excursions, mountain biking in places such as Costa Rica, Peru, Tibet, Nepal, Switzerland, and Croatia. While traveling through these very different environments and cultures—all via mountain bike—she carefully documented her experiences so she could write about and share them when she got home. The thrill was not only in the trips themselves, but also in the chance to promote the sport and build relationships.

To Elladee, mountain biking has always been a way to tap into a human need for connection. She says of her life's experience, "My passion for riding has always been the same. It wasn't just the racing that ignited the fire; it was the riding itself, the exploration and connecting with other people around the world aboard a bike. . . it opens so many doors."

Today, Elladee is stoked for her next shred, some gnarly adventure with a dialed mountain bike beneath her.

Follow Elladee Brown Online

Instagram: @elladee17

Twitter: @elladeebrown

Facebook: Elladee Brown

Lizzie Armanto:
Skateboard Wonder

Lizzie Armanto was determined to try the trick. And she not only wanted to try it, she also wanted to land it without having to bail. At first when she and her brother Max had come to the Cove Skatepark in Santa Monica, California, they had started up a friendly competition. Who could be the better skateboarder? Who could learn more tricks? But things soon changed. As Lizzie grew more and more comfortable on her board, her passion for the sport intensified. She loved discovering new tricks—and practicing until she nailed each one.

For the move she wanted to attempt that day, Lizzie had carefully watched how others performed it. *How can I do that?* she thought. She broke the trick down into each part and visualized herself doing it. She took note of the critical leg position, the timing, and how the skaters shifted their weight to drop back into the concrete bowl. She vowed to practice it for however long it took until she mastered the move.

Then she went for it.

She tried it again and again until, finally, everything worked perfectly. Leaning on her back foot, she rolled up the ramp to the top of the coping, the rim of the bowl. There she tilted her board 45 degrees, extending her front foot while keeping the back one bent and flexible. Exactly positioned, she stalled for a moment with one back wheel above the coping. With a quick glance behind her, she dropped back in, a smooth maneuver that belied its difficulty. She'd done it! She had completed a feeble fakie for the very first time!

Lizzie was born in Simi Valley, California, on January 26, 1993, to an American mother and a Finnish father. Her family soon moved to Santa Monica, where skateboarding was everywhere. Despite the sport's popularity in her community, Lizzie didn't consider trying it until she was 14. Then, skateboarding came into her life unexpectedly. Lizzie's mom was looking for an after-school outlet for her children when she asked them if they would be interested in hanging out at the Cove. They could go there directly after school and, with the kids clad in pads and helmets, it would be a supervised activity in a safe environment.

Sidewalk Surfing

Born from a desire by surfers to keep in shape when ocean conditions were poor, skateboarding was initially known as "sidewalk surfing." It was at first limited to flat surfaces such as parking lots and paved streets or sidewalks. Barefooted, people rode wooden boards made with clay wheels, the same material used for roller skates. Soon, improved technology such as polyurethane wheels made boards safer and easier to control. In 1976, a California drought helped to expand the sport further. Residents drained their swimming pools, making the empty pools the ideal spot to practice "vert," a new skateboarding style that featured climbing the vertical walls of concrete. That same year, two commercial skateparks opened, one in Florida and the other in California. As the sport became more popular, other parks opened, building half-pipes—U-shaped ramps—where skaters could perform tricks. Street-style evolved as well. This time, urban features like handrails, benches, and walls made perfect obstacles for performing various moves.

To the siblings, the skateboard park sounded like fun. At first Lizzie used a "Ninja Turtle" board that her parents had picked up from a local toy store. She hopped on the amateur board and started at square one. At the beginning, she worked on simply getting used to the sport. She practiced basic carving and feeling comfortable while she built stamina and learned to control the board. She soon moved onto to a better board; this time it was an Element.

The skate park had different sections. There was a street section where the obstacles included ledges, banks, and railings to imitate those you'd find in an urban environment. However, Lizzie preferred the pool and clover bowl. She practiced skating along the flat-bottomed dish and carving along the vert—the steep sides. At first, she didn't have the strength to climb out of the pool, but she was determined to improve. And she did. The more time Lizzie spent on her board, the more she learned and challenged herself to try different things.

Skater Style

Two basic types of skateboarding are transition and street. Transition, also referred to as "vert" for vertical, is when skaters go from a flat to a vertical surface. This can be in emptied swimming pools, in specially designed bowls, or on ramps constructed for the purpose. The top of the bowl is the table, and the rim or edge is the coping. That is where skaters can perform various tricks after dropping in and gaining enough momentum. "Park" is a subset of transition where the facility includes a series of complicated curves and steep-sided bowls. Next is street skating, which evolved from using urban obstacles such as benches, railings, or picnic tables to perform aerial tricks. If a skater does a series of consecutive tricks, the sequence is called a line. All skateboarding requires stamina, balance, and power.

Lizzie's skills got better, her hundreds of hours of training paying off. People started to notice, too. They could see that Lizzie had something special. One day she was approached by a local sponsor, SMA (Santa Monica Airlines). The representative asked if Lizzie wanted to enter a contest. She said she'd do it and immediately started thinking about the tricks she could do so she'd actually have a run. She pushed herself to learn more and to try harder tricks, setting a goal of learning a new trick every day.

The contest was the biggest bowl competition of the year, the 2009 Pro-Tec Pool Party, held in Orange, California. When Lizzie looked around, she didn't know who the pro athletes were or who was still an amateur. It was overwhelming, but Lizzie reminded herself to just skate and have fun. She stood at the top of the bowl. She waited her turn as other people snaked her—put in their boards and cut ahead of her. Feeling like a little kid, she finally went for it. She carved around the bowl and did a few tricks, feeling good and having fun. When she came in ninth and earned $200, she was stoked! She wondered if she could enter any other contests. Could she somehow make skateboarding a bigger part of her life?

It was a good time to be a female skater. Opportunities were opening up as women's events gained traction. Lizzie participated in as many contests as she could—often winning. The next year, she earned first place in the women's division of the World Cup Skateboarding championship. She picked up sponsors who supplied her with branded clothing and equipment. Whenever she won a competition, she sometimes won a small purse of money, too. During her senior year of high school, she missed a week of school when one of her sponsors paid for her ticket to Australia so she could compete in the Bondi Bowl-A-Rama. At the time, the contest had no women's division. That didn't stop Lizzie. She skated with a handful of other women and earned a respectable finish.

Lizzie applied for college, but she had no idea what she wanted to study. Nothing she did in high school resonated the way skating did. She had taken classes she thought sounded interesting, including Japanese. She joined the music program, but after trying the flute, the trombone, and some percussion instruments, she realized she didn't like the structure of practicing music. Skateboarding was different. There she was free to do whatever felt right, to challenge herself, and to go with whatever felt good at the time. The practice in skateboarding didn't feel like work. It satisfied a passion that made her crave more.

Lizzie was attending community college when she injured her knee. Unable to skate for a while, she realized just how much it meant to her. She decided to focus solely on skateboarding. Once her knee healed, Lizzie found an agent to help with the management of making this her career. Next, she signed up for as many events as she could. One day a friend texted her a picture of the popular magazine *Transworld Skateboarding*. At first, she didn't recognize the person on the cover. Then she did.

That's me, she realized. She hadn't recognized herself because it was in a bowl she'd only skated once. It was a huge honor; this was the first time *Transworld* had ever featured a woman on their cover. "It felt surreal," Lizzie mused. "I never imagined myself there." Her goal was to skate a ton and try to be as productive as possible, but nobody had asked her about the cover photo. Still, as amazing as it was to be featured on the magazine's cover, turning pro was still just a dream. Until one day it wasn't.

Lizzie was on her way to a session in Southern California in March 2017. One of her sponsors wanted to do some filming. When she biked over, she joined the vert session, skating the vertical ramp set up there. During one of the runs, she went off the side and hurt her elbow. She decided to sit down.

Jeff Grosso, a legend of the skate scene, was also there. He feigned a fall and then walked over to Lizzie on the grass. Standing in front of her, he pulled out the advance copy of *Thrasher Magazine* from where he'd hidden it under his shirt. A powerhouse publication of the skateboarding industry, the headline on the cover read "Lizzie Armanto: The Thrasher Interview." She had known about the interview, but not that she would be this month's feature article.

"Welcome to the big leagues," Jeff said, handing her the magazine. With barely time to recover from the shock, Lizzie received another surprise. This time it was Tony Hawk who stepped forward. Tony was another pioneer skateboarder and the owner of Birdhouse, a skateboard company that sponsored Lizzie. He handed her a pro-model board—her own signature board, designed by artist Kenneth Srivijittakar. Done mostly in green and pinks, the board art included things Lizzie loved—it was a breakfast scene with an octopus, eggs, and a gardenia. Lizzie was stunned beyond words. Now it was official.

Lizzie was a pro skater.

Skate and Destroy

Thrasher Magazine is an authority in skateboarding. The first edition of the magazine was published in 1981 in San Francisco, California. With the motto "Skate and Destroy," the monthly publication carries articles on all things skateboarding, including equipment and park reviews and articles on who is doing what in the skateboarding community. In 1988, Cara-Beth Burnside, an Olympian who competed in both snowboarding and skateboarding, was the first woman to be featured on the magazine's cover. *Thrasher* featured another woman on their cover in 1994. This time it was Jamie Reyes, a pro skater from Hawai'i. Lizzie's cover appeared 24 years later, for the May 2017 issue, and included a feature interview.

As a pro skateboarder, Lizzie racked up impressive statistics, winning contests and participating in various filming opportunities. She was suddenly being solicited for invitation-only events. She competed in five X Games, a twice-yearly event highlighting extreme sports and presented by the sports network ESPN. She won medals at the X Games, too—a gold for the first ever Women's Skateboard Park event in 2013, silver in 2016, and bronze in 2019. She won first place at the 2013 and 2014 Van Doren Invitationals. In 2016, skateboarding expanded its global influence with the Vans Park Series pro tour and world championships. Lizzie traveled to cities all over the globe, places such as Shanghai; Montreal; Sao Paulo; and Malmo, Sweden. The company Vans, one of her sponsors, created a "Lizzie Armanto" line of shoes and clothing.

Then, one day her sponsor and friend Tony Hawk asked her, "Hey, Lizzie, would you want to do the loop?"

The loop, nicknamed the "Loop of Death," is built like a toy car track, a 16-foot, 360-degree ramp with a 14-foot drop (4.8-m ramp, 4.3-m drop). That August, Tony's team had set it up in a parking lot in Vista, California, and had advertised the event. It drew a large crowd of spectators. Only a couple dozen people had successfully completed it—no women—and you could get seriously hurt if you didn't make it.

Before Tony's question, Lizzie had never thought about doing the loop. It was different from anything she'd ever tried before. With no experience or strategy for riding it successfully, Lizzie wasn't sure she could. Still, she was curious. She paused and then answered Tony, "I'm down to look at it if it's up, but I'm not going to commit to saying I'll do it."

The day before the event was open to the public, Lizzie went to check out Tony's loop. The structure was even more intimidating in real life. It looked bigger and taller than in the pictures. To ride it with a skateboard didn't look logical or even possible. Even with safety pads in place it was obvious that people could get hurt if they didn't do it just right . . . and people *had* gotten hurt. Lizzie shook her head. She needed to focus on the people who had been successful, those who had the technique down.

Don't pump.

Follow the line.

Lock your legs.

She forced herself not to evaluate the structure, not to have a negative opinion that would influence her outcome. Successfully riding the loop was the only conclusion.

Tony's crew removed the protective pads for the day of the actual event. With a crowd gathered and the cameras rolling, Lizzie knew that once she dropped from the top platform, she needed to totally commit. But the logistics of the run went against everything she'd learned in skateboarding. There was no exit and no reversing once you began. There was no option to bail.

Lizzie became hyper focused. She zoomed into the moment and everything outside of her immediate environment blurred. *Lean forward, but not too far forward. Lean back, but not too far back.* She didn't make it while the crowd was gathered, though thankfully she didn't get hurt. Yet, even after most people had gone home, she wasn't ready to quit. Tony agreed to keep the loop up and let Lizzie keep trying.

In the seconds before she dropped again, Lizzie went over the process of what she wanted her body to do. After five or six more attempts she made it . . . sort of. She had ridden her board all the way around the loop but then leaned back, a tiny bit too much. She fell on the roll-out after exiting the loop.

"You made it!"

But it didn't feel like it to Lizzie. She may have gone all the way around the loop, but falling in the exit didn't feel like a complete success. She climbed back to the top of the ramp. This time she rode her board around the entire loop, including a perfect roll-out!

With that triumph, Lizzie joined an exclusive list. She was the first female ever to complete Tony Hawk's famous loop.

Women in Skateboarding

In 1965, Patti McGee posed for the cover of *Life* magazine doing a handstand on a skateboard. She became the first female professional skateboarder when she was sponsored to travel around the country to demonstrate the Hobie skateboard. As the sport's popularity grew, many more men participated than women. Of the women who did skateboard, several helped to open the sport to other females.

Cara-Beth Burnside was one. She was the first president

of Action Sports Alliance, an organization formed to support female professional action-sport athletes. She also helped to convince sports network ESPN to host a women's event at the 2002 X Games. Cara-Beth advocated for equal pay to all X Game winners, regardless of gender and since 2008, this has been the X Games policy.

Today there are still more men than women who skate, but with organizations such as the Women's Skateboard Alliance and other all-female meetups, more women than ever are entering the skateboarding scene.

Today, Lizzie lives her dream. When she reflects on her rise as a pro skater, she thinks about the winding path she took to get there. There had been so many choices, so many chances to quit and do something else. But every time she thought about doing something different, Lizzie would realize how much she loved skateboarding and needed it in her life. At the beginning, when she watched experts complete difficult tricks, she doubted she'd ever be able to imitate them. But she pushed away the negative thoughts: *Am I going to make it? Is it too hard?* Instead she asked herself, *Am I making it bigger and harder than it is?*

For every skateboarding challenge, there were no guarantees that Lizzie was going to succeed. But, just like with the loop, she kept trying. When she did, suddenly something would click, and then success just happened.

"If you want to learn how to do something, you have to try and try and try," Lizzie said. "They say one of the definitions of insanity is doing the same thing over and over and expecting a different result. But in skateboarding, that's what we do and amazing things happen."

Follow Lizzie Armanto Online

Website: https://lizziearmanto.tumblr.com/

Instagram: @lizziearmanto

Twitter: @Lizziearmanto

Facebook: Lizzie Armanto

Part IV: Epic Ice and Snow

10

Kristin Knight Pace:
It's All About the Dogs

Kristin Knight Pace was in the middle of Denali National Park and Preserve, a 6 million–acre wilderness in the heart of Alaska. The sky was huge above her and Denali Peak, North America's tallest mountain, towered in the distance. She was working as a dog musher—sled dog driver—for the park service. With no motorized vehicles allowed off-road in the park, travel was with dogsleds or by foot only. She was with a team of scientists. Her mission was simple: transport the scientists and their equipment to a location deep within the park. It was supposed to be a straightforward trip, out and back. However, as Kristin has been reminded many times, nothing in Alaska is ever that simple.

When the team of scientists first approached the park service, they explained that they were studying sound pollution. They wanted to install a soundscape monitoring station about 90 miles (145 km) into the park. Unlike the southern 48 states, where it is nearly impossible to go more than 30 minutes without hearing an engine or other human-engineered sound, this section of Denali Park was going to be one of the quietest, least manmade-sound-impacted places on earth.

Along with the usual survival gear, Kristin's dogsled was loaded with science equipment. This included 50-pound (23-kg) batteries and thick glass solar panels. Despite the weight, the dogs were doing well. They were Alaskan huskies, freight-hauling dogs bred for hard work. They were strong and eager to run. In the crisp air and decent temperature, Kristin could tell that they were enjoying themselves.

The team arrived at an icy section of the Denali lowlands. It was a perfect place to set up the equipment. With less snow than in other parts of the park, the instruments were less likely to be buried or knocked over. It didn't take long for Kristin and the others to unload everything. They positioned the monitor and a microphone on a sturdy tripod. With luck, the device would be able to record one month's worth of sound—the maximum length of time the batteries and limited solar power would last.

Suddenly, just as one of the researchers was ready to turn everything on, Kristin's team of dogs burst into throaty barks. When they abruptly stopped, a few seconds later an answering volley came from across the snow. About a quarter mile away, a pack of wolves howled in return. Then they stopped, and the dogs answered. Back and forth for several minutes, the dogs and the wolves communicated in some canine, primal language that completely excluded the humans. It was a reminder of how little Kristin understood and how little she was in control. It was astonishing. It was awesome.

Long-distance dogsledding in the far north is all about the dogs. Of course, traversing hundreds of miles of trail, broken and unbroken, is also about temperatures dozens of degrees below zero, blizzards, darkness, wildlife including moose and wolves, treacherous trail hazards, windstorms so ferocious you can't tell up from down—and grit. But Kristin would say it's mostly about the dogs.

Since childhood, Kristin has always had a bond with dogs. Each has its own personality and, for her, that elevates the animals to companions, even friends. Trusting her dogs has been critical—to the point of them saving her life more than once. Although she grew up in Fort Worth, Texas, it didn't take her long to make Alaska her home. The Alaskan wilderness where she now lives in a 16-by-20-foot cabin (4.8-by-6 m), with no running water or indoor plumbing, is a place like no other. And while her dogs are part of her family, there is also something mystical and otherworldly about them.

Denali Park and Preserve

Established in 1917, Denali National Park and Preserve was the United States' first wilderness area dedicated to protecting wildlife. In 1980, an act of Congress greatly expanded its size so that the park now comprises over 6 million acres. There is only one road, with just 15 miles (24 km) of it paved and accessible by private vehicle. If you travel along the rest of the 92-mile (148-km) ribbon of mostly gravel and dirt by park bus, you will likely see plenty of wildlife. The "big five" are caribou, Dall sheep, moose, wolves, and grizzly bears—but there are a total of 39 species of mammals, 167 species of birds, and 1 species of amphibian, the wood frog.

Although spectacular to witness, the wild animals should be given a wide berth. For example, a moose, which weighs up to 1,600 pounds (725 kg), can act aggressively if stressed or tired. When hiking, avoid startling or attracting grizzly bears by making noise at regular intervals and keeping food and trash away from camps. As with all wildlife, understanding and respect for these creatures will help make most encounters positive ones.

Kristin's first experience in Alaska was during a summer internship working at the Denali Park Sled Dog Kennels. When she first took the job, a colleague described what they did like "combat mushing." The conditions were frequently daunting. Often the snow was too deep even for the dogs. When that happened, Kristin would have to break in a trail using snowshoes in front of the team. She and her dogs also had to regularly navigate a path over or around downed trees.

They frequently had to bushwhack through hearty willows and other vegetation, with Kristin working to make sure the dogs' lines didn't get hung up or tangled. In the right conditions, sled dogs can cover 100 miles a day. During the internship, sometimes Kristin and her team were lucky to go ten.

At the end of that summer, Kristin drove south with two treasures—a newfound respect for Alaska and a six-week-old puppy from the latest litter at the Denali National Park sled dog kennels. She named him Moose. When she had the opportunity to move back to Alaska a few years later, she didn't hesitate. At the time, solitude and a focus on simple living was exactly what she needed—surprisingly, she didn't end up with either.

"There are eight dogs. You can have a free place to stay if you look after them while I'm away," the owner of the cabin told her.

A friend from Alaska had put Kristin in touch with a man looking for someone to take care of his sled dogs for the winter. Feeling the tug of the north, Kristin and her two dogs (she'd introduced Moose to a stray she adopted named Maximus) arrived at James's cabin at the beginning of November. Her new home was small and had only the basics. No bathroom inside meant using an outhouse. There was no running water, either, so showers were once a week at a neighbor's house. There was no need for a refrigerator, James explained before he left. He showed her the trapdoor in the floor opening to a natural "cold hole" below the cabin floor. Nearer the top was where she could put things that needed to be cold, but not frozen. Deeper in the hole where the ground was permanently frozen was where she should store items she wanted to freeze. It was perfect.

That winter in James's cabin, Kristin found a kind of freedom that she had never experienced anywhere else. There were fewer rules and regulations. And to survive, people needed to be self-reliant. Yes, it could be lonely, but there was no freer place she knew of.

At first Kristin took the dogs—hers and James's—for daily walks in a large, roaming pack. She didn't try harnessing them to a dogsled until she'd been in the cabin for a couple of months. Then, remembering what she'd learned during her internship at the kennels, she managed to attach each dog to a gangline, the leash that connects the dogs to the sled. When every animal was in place, she untied the knot she had secured to a fence post. The sled lurched forward as the dogs flew across the snow farther and faster than they'd ever been with Kristin. It was scary. It was exhilarating. She couldn't wait to do it again.

The first time Kristin thought about running in an actual sled dog race was when she was watching the start of the Yukon Quest, a 1,000-mile (1,600-km) contest held every year in February. The power of the 300-plus dogs at the starting gate was electric. As each sled driver let go of a metal brake on his or her sled, the dog teams pitched forward, the force of their energy shooting them ahead as if they were one entity. For the next several days, each team of dogs and one human would survive on a wilderness trail that was as dangerous as it was breathtaking.

Sled Dogs: Made for Cold

Humans survive during extreme cold with carefully engineered clothing and modern equipment. Sled dogs rely on natural adaptations to thrive in subzero temperatures. First is their double layer of fur. The undercoat is soft and thick, while the overcoat consists of long, stiff guard hairs that are water-resistant. This hair doesn't lie flat, either, which creates a thick layer of insulation. The dogs' otherwise vulnerable paws contain freeze-resistant fat and tissue. Also, a system of closely packed veins and arteries brings warm blood to the region, helping dogs walk or run for miles on ice and snow without getting frostbite. Sled dogs sleep outside. To guard against subzero temperatures, they wrap themselves in a ball to decrease surface area and then cover their vulnerable nose and mouth with their thick, furry tails.

When Kristin's first winter ended, she decided to stay in Alaska. It was serendipity when she got a call soon after her decision to stay—would she like a temporary job as a backcountry ranger for the Denali Park Service? *Absolutely*, Kristin thought. It was a dream job.

The park service used sled dogs for transportation, but racing wasn't on Kristin's radar until the next winter. She had signed up to volunteer for the Iditarod, a sled dog race similar to the Yukon Quest, but bigger and with more contestants and more media coverage. Kristin's assignment was at the Nikolai checkpoint, one of several locations where teams passed through on the multiday race. As she watched each of the participants come in, she noted how the mushers would take just a few minutes to feed their dogs and bed them down on straw spread over the snow. With the dogs taken care of, they took a quick nap themselves and then were off to run another leg of the race. It was thrilling to watch. Not only, that, it was *doable*. Kristin felt a knot of desire growing. *I could do this*, she told herself.

Kristin had a new goal. Somehow, she was going to figure out a way to run in the Iditarod.

Mush! The Iditarod Sled Dog Race

In 1967, Alaska celebrated the hundred-year anniversary of its purchase from Russia. To honor the occasion, a committee organized a 56-mile (90-km) sled dog race along the Iditarod trail, the main transportation route used by settlers during Alaska's gold rush in the 1890s and early 1900s.

Years later, in 1973, interest sparked for another sled dog race. Named after the trail, this was the official start to today's Iditarod. The first winner of this grueling, 1,000-mile race (1,610 km) was Dick Wilmarth—and he took three weeks to complete the course. In 1985, Libby Riddles was the first woman to win the Iditarod. She did it in 18 days, 20 minutes, and 17 seconds.

Today, while top contenders finish in under ten days, those days are full of unbelievable challenges. Unpredictable weather and bone-chilling temperatures aside, mushers take little time to sleep and can experience extreme fatigue. Some people name it the most difficult race on earth.

Training for a long-distance sled dog race requires many steps and often years of preparation. The first thing Kristin needed was a team of dogs. She had met and married a like-minded man named Andy. Together, they bought their first sled dog puppies and opened a racing dog kennel, which they named Hey, Moose! Kennel, after Kristin's beloved first dog. She also bought Solo, an older and already established sled dog. As soon as the puppies were old enough, Kristin began training them—and herself. To run in a race like the Iditarod, she would need to anticipate every life-or-death situation on the long, isolated trail between checkpoints. Preparation could mean the difference between survival and death.

Puppies to Team Dogs

Training puppies to run as sled dogs starts from an early age. From as young as three months old, puppies are let loose to run beside the older dogs tethered to a sled. They continue this free running until they begin to insert themselves into gaps in the line of dogs. *Where* the dogs insert themselves is also an indication of the role they will play in the team. If a puppy chooses to always run in front, they may end up being a lead dog. The other positions are swing dogs, those directly behind the lead and who help with steering around corners; team dogs who are the main force of the team; and wheel dogs, those directly in front of the sled. Aside from running practice, puppies need to be socialized, too. With a race like the Iditarod, there are thousands of fans watching and hundreds of vets and other personnel on hand. Dogs must be coached to get used to being around a lot of people. Training includes a ton of love, such as touching and handling.

As the puppies grew up, Kristin and Andy bred them with other dogs. Soon they had a viable team of sled dogs. Now Kristin needed to work on qualifying for the Iditarod. According to the rules sheet, only those mushers who have raced in certain other mid-distance or long-distance races and have proven themselves capable are eligible to enter this pinnacle race. Kristin built up a combined 650 miles (1,050 km) of mid-distance sled dog races. She thought she was set, but when she went to fill out the application for the Iditarod, she realized she was 150 miles (240 km) short. At first she was devastated. Then she signed up for the Yukon Quest.

Though less well known than the Iditarod, the Yukon Quest is every bit as difficult and, in some respects, more challenging than its sister race. It takes place each year in February, a month earlier than the Iditarod. Colder and with less daylight, the Yukon Quest has fewer checkpoints, too. Mushers need to carry more food and equipment and therefore have heavier sleds.

It was −40 degrees Fahrenheit (−40°C) on February 7, 2015, in Whitehorse, Canada, when Kristin attached booties to each dog on her team. The booties were necessary to protect the dogs' paws over the course of the race, and Kristin would have to replace them several times. Next, she attached each dog to the gangline as excitement and fear flowed through her. Now that she was actually here, how was she going to pull this off?

Then she was off, the sled careening through the wilderness, with the dogs much more in charge of where they were going than Kristen. On the back of the sled, her full concentration was directly ahead of her. Was everyone running smoothly? Were there any issues? Were all the booties still on securely? Did any dogs have a snowball stuck in their paws?

Each of the dogs had to take in 10,000 or more calories every day; Kristin would need to feed them frequently. At various points along the trail, she passed out chunks of salmon and other snacks. At each checkpoint, there was no time to relax, either. She heated water to add to kibble and meat to feed the team. Then she laid down a bed of hay so they could rest. After assessing the dogs to make sure each was still in peak condition, she powered down a quick meal herself before snatching far too little sleep.

The hazards of the trail for both races—the Yukon Quest and the Iditarod—include intense weather and temperatures. The Yukon Quest was deathly cold the year Kristin ran it, while the Iditarod's trail the next year was barren of snow for hundreds of miles. Other dangers included scaling mountains, running on partially frozen rivers, sometimes over jagged ice, and encountering wildlife. So many times, the dogs—not Kristin—determined the outcome of a situation, especially Solo.

There's a reason Solo has his name. Kristin has often had to trust him to make the big decisions alone. While he might start acting up during the boring, well-marked trails by veering off, or even stopping to pee on trees, Kristin knows she can count on him during the most extreme, scariest parts: "Glare ice, no sign of a trail. That's his bread and butter. He wants to be super challenged."

During the Iditarod, Solo's actions averted certain disaster during an encounter with a wood bison. The team was racing through a section of the trail called the burn. The snow had given way to dirt. It was a dust-choked, miserable ride. In a second, the situation got worse. An adult wood bison, weighing at least 2,000 pounds (910 kg), stopped sideways directly in front of the team. The sled's brake was useless without snow and, besides, the dogs had no interest in slowing down.

Crash! The team collided with the massive animal, leaping onto its flank until it shook them off and ran into the woods. Every dog but Solo turned to follow the bison, a decision that would mean certain disaster. Mercifully, Solo's stubborn adherence to continuing straight ahead on the trail won over the rest of the dogs. Solo had just saved them all.

Kristin finished the Iditarod in 11 days, 13 hours, 31 minutes, and 32 seconds. She arrived in Nome, Alaska, in 58th place out of a total of 85 mushers, including 14 who had quit partway through. Of those who finished, Kristin was one of 16 rookies. Running the 975 miles (1,570 km) had been dangerous, exhausting, risky—and beautiful. It was life changing and life affirming. "One thing I love about Alaska is there isn't anyone watching you," Kristen said. "There is no judgment. There you are free to pick the thing you love and really go for it."

When Kristin thought back to the near misses, she always came back to the power of the dogs. The more they raced, the more powerful they became, gaining energy instead of losing it. Kristin reflected on her human self. The Iditarod had drained her, mentally and physically. She was ecstatic that she had finished, but she also felt distinctly that she had, many times, just been along for the ride. The dogs were the heroes. They were the ones who knew, who thrived, who were in control. Kristin thanked them. She loved them. They were her family and they had brought her home.

Follow Kristin Knight Pace Online

Website: www.heymoosekennel.com

Instagram: @kristinknightpace

Twitter: @HeyMooseKennel

Julia Marino:
The Art of Snowboarding

The conditions were perfect at the Laax Resort in the heart of Switzerland. It was 30 degrees Fahrenheit (−1°C) and sunny, with compact snow. In bib number three and wearing a helmet featuring the Mountain Dew logo, Julia Marino was there to compete in the Laax Open Snowboard World Cup, sponsored by the International Ski Federation. Her event was slopestyle. During the 1,640-foot (500-m) run, she would be snowboarding down an obstacle course that included challenging rails and jumps. This freestyle terrain was Julia's specialty. After placing eighth at yesterday's qualifier, today Julia planned to perform her best tricks—hoping to impress the panel of judges.

It wasn't the first time Julia had participated in the Laax Open. For the last two years she had earned fourth-place finishes. This year she hoped to move up to a podium finish. But how? The competition was intense. The other women who had qualified were world experts, powerful athletes who had been training their whole lives. Julia, on the other hand, didn't start seriously snowboarding until well into her teens.

The course contained six sections, each with multiple obstacles. Julia planned her route carefully. She analyzed each feature and worked out the tricks she would perform on each one. Her strategy was always the same: she visualized each move before she dropped into the course. The sequence would be like the sketches she loved to draw in her free time. Each section flowed into the whole picture.

At the top of the course, Julia was seconds away from the start of her first run. Each athlete got two chances to complete the course, and the better of the two counted toward the final score. Julia knew she needed to start strong. Competition was as much a mental game as it was about performing well physically. If she messed up initially, she might not have the mindset to do well the second time.

Julia put on her gloves. Unlike many of the other athletes, she did not play music while in competition. She wanted to be aware of everything around her and that included the sound of her board on snow. She was off!

She popped over the front jump, rotating so her right foot was forward, a stance called goofy foot. She hopped onto a rail, riding it backward until swinging around to face down the hill. The next obstacle involved a cylinder-shaped feature nicknamed the cannon. Here her landing included a spin in the air. She nailed it! Now she focused on building speed. The following trick was the hardest yet, and she would need significant momentum to pull it off.

Julia's run up to the jump was fast and straight. At the lip of the hurdle, she flipped backward in a back 900 melon—an air somersault, rotating two and a half times. She landed perfectly. There was no time to celebrate. At the next jump Julia propelled herself upward, executing a double-under flip, one hand grabbing her board to help curl her body. When she landed, she faced one last obstacle, another jump that she again approached with control and power. Another flip and she was done with the course.

Yes! Julia pumped her arm. She had to wait for the judges' scores, but the run had felt *good*. Not only that, it had been fun!

When Julia won the 2020 Laax Open, standing on the top spot of the podium was almost surreal. Beside her were top performers Reira Iwabuchi from Japan and Katie Ormerod from Great Britain, both incredibly talented snowboarders. Julia was a long way from her Westport, Connecticut, home where, when she was a child, her family took ski trips once a year. Julia hadn't even liked snowboarding at first. If circumstances hadn't forced her hand, she may never have strapped one on. She may never have joined Team USA or secured sponsors such as Mountain Dew, Dragon, Burton, or StaminaPro. If not for one fateful day with a broken ski, Julia may never have gone pro in snowboarding, traveling the globe and competing in world-class events.

Julia was born in 1997. It was evident early on that she was an exceptional athlete. At the age of two and a half, she was already riding a two-wheel bicycle. A few years later she started going down steep hills on her bike, sometimes with no hands. When Julia was in kindergarten, her parents got a phone call. Somehow Julia had scaled a wall—could they please tell her not to do it again?

Young Julia also liked jumping off things. She climbed trees and loved to spend time at the playground. She craved activity and sports were a huge part of her life. From an early age, she played on a soccer team that her dad helped coach.

A Marino family tradition was a once-a-year ski trip to Colorado. Every February, the family would spend ten days in the mountains, the only time all year Julia got to go skiing. On one of these trips, when she was seven years old, Julia was riding the chairlift up the slope with her dad. "Dad, I've got a surprise for you," she said to him.

Once off the lift, she led her dad to a ski jump. Young Julia gathered speed and then flew off the top, landing solidly on her skis on the other side. She couldn't wait to do it again.

The trips to Colorado always involved skiing, but one year Julia's parents bought her a snowboard as a gift. They brought it along on the family trip, and Julia tried it out. She wasn't a fan. She was better at skiing and saw no reason to switch to something new. She set the snowboard aside . . . until she broke one of her skis.

At age 11, Julia was an advanced skier. She often avoided the groomed, intermediate slopes and instead preferred to ski between the trees or on more challenging terrain, the more obstacles and jumps the better. She was between the trees one day and skiing pretty hard when one ski broke.

"Dad, can I just rent another pair?" she asked. But her dad said no. He reminded her of the perfectly good snowboard sitting inside their rented condo. Julia was not happy. She didn't want to spend the whole vacation snowboarding. She wasn't good at it. How was she going to enjoy the rest of the trip if she didn't have access to skis? Grumbling, she strapped on the snowboard. Then something happened. Surprising herself—but maybe not the rest of her family—she was commanding the snowboard in no time, taking on obstacles and enjoying airtime off jumps. Suddenly it *was* fun. Maybe there was something to snowboarding after all. . . .

Snurfer to Snowboard

In 1965, Sherman Poppen created a new activity for his kids by fastening two skis together. Combining skiing, surfing, and skateboarding, the Poppens called it snurfing. The idea took off. As about a million snurfers sold over the next few years, innovators improved upon the design. Closer to the modern snowboard was the winterstick, a single board invented by surfer Dimitrije Milovich.

Soon competitions popped up. The first national snow

surfing contest took place in 1982. Finally, in 1994, the Olympic committee recognized the sport and included it in the 1998 Olympic games in Nagano, Japan. Today, snowboarding includes several subdisciplines and is popular throughout the world.

The Marinos could see that Julia was athletically gifted. It was impossible not to notice that her skills were superior to casual snowboarders her age (and older ones, too). Others were taking note, too. People at the mountain came up to Julia's parents, commenting on Julia's skill. It was clear that she could take snowboarding further—if she wanted to.

Julia was around 12 years old when her parents asked her, "Are you interested in doing more?" If she wanted to get serious about the sport, maybe train and enter a few amateur competitions, she would need lessons. Maybe even a coach.

"Yeah, I think so," Julia answered.

Her dad called up the ski school at the mountain. "My daughter might have a talent," he said tentatively, completely understating the obvious. Soon, Julia and her dad met an instructor at the bottom of the lift. The instructor began the lesson slowly—too easy and too boring. Julia looked for the first thing she could find to jump off. The instructor took one look and then led Julia and her dad off-trail.

At the end of the lesson, the instructor shook his head. "Girls aren't doing this stuff," he said in amazement. He told the two of them about a winter sports academy called Stratton Mountain

School. It was a boarding school located in southern Vermont. The school trained pro athletes and even future Olympians. Most important, they had a snowboarding program.

Flips, Blunts, and Cabs

Spaghetti, pretzel, roast beef, melon—this sounds like the lineup at an all-you-can-eat buffet. It's not. Along with bus driver, McTwist, and cab, these snowboarding trick names are like another language.

Slopestyle is a subdiscipline of snowboarding in which riders run a course of six to eight features with as much style and originality as possible. Judges score each maneuver according to its technical difficulty, how well it was executed, and the overall flow. Slopestyle tricks include jumps, grabs, spins, flips, and slides, and most can be done in combination with others. The degree of rotation is added to the name of the trick as well. For example, a 360 means someone completed one full 360-degree turn. Two rotations would be a 720. Grabs also have different names, depending on where they are on the snowboard and which hand is doing it. This is where melon, roast beef, and chicken salad come in. But not all these moves are named after food. A nose grab, for example, is when the rider grips the nose, or front of the board.

The next step for the Marinos was to make an appointment at the Stratton Mountain School. After a quick demonstration on the slopes, they followed the head coach to his office. "She's ready," the coach said. "We'll take her right now." He turned to Julia and tossed her a sports drink. "How would you like to be on that bottle some day?"

To leave home and live at the academy was a huge commitment. At first Julia opted to do just a weekend program. The Marinos worked out a compromise with her school back home. If Julia was willing to come in 45 minutes early every day to work with her teachers, the principal at Bedford Middle School would authorize her to take Fridays off so her dad could drive her to Stratton. Yes! This was exactly what Julia wanted to do.

Julia's skills improved. Soon she was competing in amateur competitions—and winning. But back home she was doing well, too. She was playing soccer; in her freshman year at St. Joseph High School in Trumbull, Connecticut, she was a star player. But she had a decision to make. She loved snowboarding, but she wasn't sure she wanted to give up soccer to live at Stratton full time. Again, the Marinos worked out a solution. Both schools agreed that Julia could stay home to play out the soccer season at St. Joseph's. The day after the last game ended, Julia headed north to Stratton for the winter.

Tenth grade was more of the same. This time, though, Julia finished soccer season at home, then went out west for the winter. The East Coast (Ice Coast, as Julia referred to it) just didn't have the same snow conditions as the mountains out west. The team at Stratton Mountain School arranged for a coach to train Julia and two boys in Breckenridge Ski Resort in Colorado. This process continued during her junior year—soccer in the fall and snowboarding when the season was over.

Next, Julia joined the Ski and Snowboard Club of Vail, another Colorado resort with mountain terrain challenging enough for her advanced skill level. Unfortunately, the program was disorganized and instead of helping Julia progress in the sport, it was stressful and confusing. This was supposed to be fun. Julia was supposed to be getting expert training to help make her better.

Julia and her dad had a heart-to-heart talk. Should she quit and focus on soccer? Her team at school was undefeated that year. Julia had already received scholarship offers to play Division 1 soccer at college. Should she accept one of the offers and head to college after graduating?

There was an alternative. Julia had worked with a coach, Max Henault, in Quebec over the summer doing some dryland training—athletic exercises to get ready for snowboarding, mostly using a trampoline. Should they reach out to Max and see if he could take Julia on? To Julia, choosing snowboarding over soccer was a no-brainer, if it was an option.

"When do you want to start?" her dad asked her.

"Tomorrow."

Max *was* available to train Julia. He could start as soon as she could get up there. Julia and her dad packed up their belongings and drove the three days to Quebec. It was exactly the right decision. Under Max's training schedule, Julia's progression in the sport greatly accelerated. By the end of that season, she was invited to join the US Ski and Snowboarding Team. It was a move that changed everything.

Making the Team

Established in 1905, the US Ski and Snowboarding Association's (USSA) mission is to "lead, encourage and support athletes in achieving excellence by empowering national teams, clubs, coaches, parents, official volunteers, and fans." Their purpose is to help athletes develop into best-in-the-world Olympic athletes. The organization supports seven disciplines in skiing and snowboarding. There are currently 11 athletes on the pro slopestyle snowboarding team. Members of the team join by invitation only, but once on the team, they have access to support such as coaches and facilities. The USSA maintains a state-of-the-art training facility in Park City, Utah, that all team members have access to.

"List some of your top accomplishments," read one question in the packet Julia received from Team USA. She was stumped. Her family suggested she list some of the wins she'd had—a lot—and some of the tricks she had by now mastered.

"Yeah, but that's bragging," she exclaimed. Julia recognized her wins, but she knew she had a long way to go if she was going to be a professional snowboarder.

It was now impossible to play soccer in the fall and limit snowboarding to just the winter. Even attending regular school hours was too much. Julia said goodbye to her team and to her school. She poured herself into snowboarding, completing her senior year of high school through online courses.

Though Julia was doing very well in a number of nationwide events, she didn't have enough points to qualify for the bigger, more prestigious competitions. That is, not until the Polartec Big Air event at Fenway Park. Originally, Julia wasn't supposed to participate. She was attending the competition as an alternate, which meant that she would maybe get in a practice run or two before the official opening but would not take part in the actual contest. It was going to be a fun, low-stress couple of days.

Julia arrived on Wednesday, February 10, 2016, stepping for her first time into the iconic park in the middle of Boston. She took in the manmade ramp built in the middle of the 103-year-old ballpark. Big air meant that there was one jump—a 140-foot (43-m) tall and 430-foot (130-m) long structure covered in snow. Each snowboarder would do three runs, earning points for each jump. The person with the highest score would claim the win. There were a lot of top athletes participating, and Julia hoped to see some fantastic trick performances.

Then, Julia's status changed. A competitor had gotten hurt, and now Julia was needed to take her place. Tomorrow, Julia *would* be a contestant. Suddenly nervous, Julia told herself to stay calm. She reminded herself that she had completed each trick many, many times in practice. Of course, it was never before on a ramp like this—or in front of nearly 12,000 fans.

It was dark when Julia stood at the top of the ramp, her nerves threatening to overpower the concentration she needed to complete the trick. It was super windy, too, and it felt like the whole structure was swaying. She took a deep breath of the frigid air. She was here now; there was no way to back out. Julia raced down the icy ramp. Her underflip was smooth, and though the track was slick, she landed it well. The jump had felt good, and when the judges submitted her score, Julia realized that she had a chance to win.

With her next two jumps at the Fenway Park event, Julia, who had been relatively unknown before this, did win. Her life exploded. She received invitations to compete at the highest levels including the X Games where, from 2017 to 2019, she won seven metals: one gold, three silver, and three bronze.

Julia set her sights on the Olympics, too. When she qualified for the 2018 games, she headed to Pyeongchang, South Korea. For the first time, the Olympic committee had added a big-air event, after including slopestyle in 2014. Julia participated in both, earning a very respectable 10th and 11th place.

Today, Julia travels all over the world to places like Switzerland, Italy, the Czech Republic, China, Japan, New

Zealand, and throughout the US and Canada. She recently bought a house in Quebec, near the training facility where she works to perfect her moves when she's not competing. Julia works hard to stay ahead of her game, living by the motto "Luck is at the intersection of hard work and opportunity."

When she's not training or competing, Julia loves to draw, take photos, or spend time with her family and her dog. What's next for this amazing athlete? As long as it involves snow, a snowboard, and interesting terrain features, Julia is ready to drop in.

Follow Julia Marino Online

Website: www.tsu.social/juliamarino

Instagram: @_juliamarino

Twitter: @julia_marino

Facebook: Julia Marino

Angela Hawse:
Alpine Adventurer

The AStar B3 helicopter was fueled up and ready to fly. A pilot and four other passengers plus a guide would fill the space inside. That meant that everyone's skis and backpacks would be transported in a ski basket attached to the side of the helicopter. At the landing site on top of the mountain with the helicopter still running, the guide would unload the passengers and equipment.

Today, Angela Hawse was that guide. But it wasn't the skis or backpacks she was most concerned about—she needed to make sure that each passenger understood her safety instructions before they began the expedition. The day was supposed to be fun, but it could also be dangerous if you weren't prepared for the risks involved. As the certified heli-skiing guide, it was Angela's job to make sure everyone stayed alive.

Angela went through the items that were packed for today's adventure. Each client had a set of poles and fat skis, perfect for the pristine powder snow conditions on the upper slopes of the mountain. For safety, Angela made sure everyone had their own transceiver and knew how to use the device that would send a location signal should anyone be buried in an avalanche. In addition, every skier carried an avalanche airbag. If someone *was* caught in a snow slide, this could mean the difference between life and death. The manually deployed device would inflate a large, balloon-type structure attached to a backpack. Since larger objects rise to the top during an avalanche, this would increase a person's chances of ending up near the surface.

Angela also had each skier carry a portable shovel and a probe in their backpacks. The probe was an expandable pole for helping to locate a buried victim. As an avalanche forecaster, Angela monitored the snow conditions constantly. However, despite her expertise at interpreting the safety of a slope, avalanches could still happen unexpectedly. Being prepared and having the right equipment saved lives. Angela knew—she had been on rescue missions before.

Mountain Safety: Off-Piste

While many skiers enjoy the groomed trails of mountain resorts, off-piste means getting into unmonitored backcountry. Heli-skiers gain access to remote mountain slopes where the snow is untouched by other skiers and the scenery is breathtaking. While the sport is generally safe, avalanches do happen occasionally. Anyone who has spent time in the mountains knows to look for the signs of unstable snow. An experienced alpinist will gauge the conditions on any slope with an incline of more than 25 degrees to determine if it's safe to ski on it. Avoiding a dangerous situation is always the best defense. Next is the rule of never skiing alone. If someone *is* accidentally caught in an avalanche, the weight of the snow on top of them acts like a mass of cement. Rescuers have up to 15 minutes to find and dig that person out—suffocation is the leading cause of death during an avalanche. Other mountain hazards include inclement weather, tree wells—holes found around trees—crevasses, or deep canyons that can be masked by snow.

Satisfied that she had loaded all of their equipment, Angela climbed into the helicopter last. As the machine climbed, she looked over the stunning landscape. The day was perfect; an icy blue sky made a dramatic contrast to the pristine snow on top of the mountain. As the helicopter touched down and the passengers unloaded, Angela felt the familiar thrill of adventure calling her. No matter how many times she guided a group for an excursion in the mountains, it never got old. Every day was a spectacular opportunity to enjoy the great, expansive beauty of the backcountry.

"We'll go one at a time," Angela told her group after assessing the slope. Her evaluation indicated good stability, but there was no reason to expose more than one person at a time to the hazard of triggering an avalanche.

"Who's going first?"

Angela grew up in a small town in the Allegheny Mountains of West Virginia. She enjoyed an idyllic childhood and spent most of it outside. Every day there was an adventure awaiting her in the forest and rivers that surrounded her home. She loved to climb trees and grapevines and go exploring. She frequently suited up with a helmet and shoulder pads so she could play tackle football with her cousins and other neighborhood boys. As long as she was active, she was happy.

When she was younger, Angela wasn't sure what she wanted to do with her life. She never envisioned that she would become a top-rated mountain guide, not only leading local heli-skiing trips, but climbing and trekking throughout the United States and the world. She never imagined she would join expeditions to famous mountain peaks such as Everest, Denali, and Aconcagua in Argentina. Nor did she ever see herself as the president of the country's leading organization for mountaineering, the American Mountain Guides Association (AMGA). One thing she did know, however, was that she was passionate about the outdoors.

While taking a geology course after she graduated from high school, Angela suddenly became intrigued by the makeup of rocks and outdoor terrain. She decided to transfer to a small college in Arizona to pursue her love for outdoor education. She still had no idea what she wanted to do with her life, but Prescott College seemed like a step in the right direction.

The first thing she noticed at the college was that all her professors were happy. Really happy. All outdoor enthusiasts themselves, it was pretty clear that whatever they were doing was giving them great joy. Angela wanted a similar path. Soon she was climbing rocks, rafting down rivers, winter camping, and backcountry skiing. She learned outdoor survival skills, such as how to make a fire and how to camp in the woods. This was exactly what she wanted to do. Angela learned more valuable outdoor skills when she worked for Outward Bound and then as an adjunct professor for Prescott College after she graduated. She became a huge advocate for protecting the outdoors and began incorporating service projects in whatever she did.

Gaining experience and knowledge, Angela soon had opportunities to guide expeditions all over the world. In the late 1990s, she helped make history when she was the deputy leader for an expedition to Mount Everest.

Tom Whittaker was a colleague at Prescott. He was also an amputee. When he was younger, a car accident had taken his right foot and the section of his leg below his knee. He wore a prosthetic, a flexible piece of plastic and metal that helped him walk. Before teaming up with Angela, he had tried to summit Everest twice but failed. The first time he had to stop because of altitude sickness and frostbite. The second time his oxygen supply ran low. Still, this time he was confident he could do it. If he could just gather enough money for the expedition through fundraisers, he desperately wanted to try it again. If he succeeded in climbing to Everest's summit, he would be the first amputee to have done it.

Tom got the money. Now he needed Angela's help.

Everest: Mother Goddess of the Earth

The Tibetan name for Mount Everest is Chomolungma, "Mother Goddess of the Earth." Located between Nepal and Tibet, it is the highest pinnacle on earth, towering 29,035 feet (8,850 m) above sea level. Each year, hundreds of people attempt to reach its summit during a small window of opportunity when the weather cooperates. On May 29, 1953, Edmund Hillary and Tenzing Norgay, part of a British expedition, were the first team to summit the mountain. Others had tried before them but failed, either aborting the attempt or dying on the mountain.

It is incredibly dangerous to climb Mount Everest for many reasons, including harsh weather, subzero temperatures, and lack of oxygen at the higher altitudes. Often, modern climbers bring supplemental oxygen with them as they ascend beyond 25,000 feet (7,620 m), the altitude known as the "death zone" because of the thin air.

To date, over 5,000 people have successfully summited the mountain. In 1975, Japanese Junko Tabei became the first woman to reach the top. The first successful American woman to summit was Stacy Allison in 1988. Then, in 2016 Melissa Arnot Reid made history as the first American female to survive the ascent and descent without using supplemental oxygen. She has summitted Everest six times in nine attempts.

When Angela signed on to help lead the Everest project, she was working on getting her master's degree. She was also teaching at Prescott College. Seeing the terrific opportunity the Everest expedition would provide, she invited four of her undergrad students to participate in a service-learning project. Angela and her students spent the semester learning about the mountain. Where was it? What were some of its unique challenges? What about the surrounding communities—what could they learn about the culture of the people who lived in the area? Angela was interested in how the impact of tourism and the popularity of the mountain had affected the lives of these people. After studying what they could from the United States, the next step was to fly to Kathmandu.

When Angela joined the Everest team, she had plenty of other climbing experience, including mountaineering in Nepal. On those trips, one thing she had noticed was the amount of litter that had accumulated on some of the mountains. During the six-week long project on Everest, Angela worked with her team of Sherpa—members of a group of locals renowned for their mountaineering skills—to remove 100 discarded oxygen bottles and about 2,000 pounds (910 kg) of trash. The undergrad students, meanwhile, worked on service projects throughout the Khumbu Valley.

Tom's summit attempt itself was a huge team effort. While it is extraordinarily difficult for anyone to reach the summit of Everest, Tom's disability made it even more challenging. He fitted a boot sole on the bottom of his prosthetic foot and added crampons—a gripping device used by climbers to improve traction. However, the artificial foot provided other complications. In the harsh conditions of the climb, Tom lost weight, and his prosthetic no longer fit properly. That made it uncomfortable to wear and difficult to control. Tom, however, didn't let that stop him.

Most of the time, Angela climbed with Tom. They started at Base Camp and ascended and descended in a staggered process meant to help acclimate them to the thinning oxygen higher on the mountain. They would need to function in an atmosphere of about 40 percent less oxygen than what you find at sea level. Each time they climbed a little higher, they built up the strength needed to survive the top of the mountain. After weeks of acclimatizing, finally, it was time to make a summit attempt.

The first time the weather allowed them to, Angela and another team member climbed to the South Summit, an elevation of 28,704 feet (8,749 m) above sea level and just a few hundred feet lower than Everest's primary peak. Tom wasn't with them. He had fallen ill and was too sick to join them. From the South Summit, Angela and her climbing partner would have to trek single file along a narrow ridge called the Cornice Traverse. The route was the most exposed section of the climb, with a more than 10,000-foot (3,050-m) drop on either side. After that was the Hillary Step, a short rock tower where climbing ropes were necessary. While not technically challenging for experienced climbers like Angela, every minute they spent in the death zone was risky. Along with the problem of low oxygen concentrations, at dozens of degrees below zero, the two of them would have to keep moving. If they stopped for long, they would soon literally freeze.

At the South Summit, hurricane force winds suddenly began building around them. Their window of good weather had ended. Now Angela and her partner had two choices: try to continue onto Everest's peak or descend immediately—and live. They reversed their climb; Angela didn't know if she would have another opportunity at the summit, but she did know it wasn't worth dying for.

A week later, when the weather cleared up enough to stay safe, Tom decided to try for the peak one last time. Alongside four Sherpa guides, he succeeded in reaching Everest's summit. With this success, he became the first person with a disability to reach the highest point on earth.

After the Everest expedition, Angela's guiding opportunities expanded. In the summers she led rock-climbing expeditions.

During the winter months she was mostly involved with back-country skiing, heli-skiing, and some ice-climbing. She spent as much time as she could outside while earning more skills and recognition.

The American Mountain Guides Association (AMGA) is an organization that trains and certifies aspiring mountain guides and climbing instructors in the United States. The global counterpart is the International Federation of Mountain Guides Associations (IFMGA). Today there are only a handful of women who are AMGA and IFMGA certified. Angela was the sixth woman ever to earn this designation in the United States and the first to join the association's instructor team. She was also the first female to become an instructor for AMGA in all three areas: rock, alpine, and ski guiding. It wasn't surprising that in 2011 AMGA awarded Angela with their "Guide of the Year" award.

Women and Climbing

Throughout the ages, people have felt the lure of mountain climbing. In 1857 in London, England, the world's first mountaineering club opened its doors—but it was for men only. Despite the negative stigma of being a female climber, several women bucked tradition and took up the sport. Many did it while wearing cumbersome dresses and skirts since it was frowned upon—even illegal—for women to wear pants.

Fanny Bullock Workman, a pioneer in women's climbing, spent her whole career climbing in bulky dresses. Despite this restriction, she broke several altitude records for women. She was also a fierce advocate for women's rights, and one photo shows her posing on a glacier in the Himalayas holding a newspaper with the headline "VOTES FOR WOMEN."

Another woman of the day, Annie Smith Peck, completed other high-altitude climbs. However, her accomplishments were overshadowed in the media by the fact that she wore trousers instead of a dress. Both Workman and Peck were founding members of the American Alpine Club.

Angela's experiences in the mountains have not always been positive. Though she has never been caught in an avalanche herself or had a serious accident on the mountain, many times she has been involved in the rescue of others. One such time was when she was climbing Mount Fitz Roy in Argentina.

Mount Fitz Roy, known as Cerro Chaltén to locals, is located in the Patagonia region between Argentina and Chile. Angela was on a three-week expedition to climb it. She and her climbing partner had met another team earlier at base camp, but then lost track of them on the mountain. Suddenly, the weather turned vicious. Angela and her partner hunkered down in a snow cave to ride out the storm. She was snug in her cold weather sleeping bag when a man stumbled into their camp and woke them up. His friend, he explained, had fallen over a thousand feet. They had been descending a rock face by rappelling with their rope. The anchor attached to the rock had failed, and the man's friend had plummeted out of control to the bottom of the rock face. Although unconscious, the man was pretty sure his friend was alive. For now.

Angela got organized. She packed up a stove and sleeping bags and sent another climbing team down the mountain to get help. She and her partner followed the man back to where his friend had fallen and assessed the situation. First they had to locate the man—who remained unresponsive—and then lower him off a steep slope, ensuring that nobody else fell or got hurt. It was a slow and careful process over the course of one and a half days. Ultimately, the victim of the fall made a full recovery, though he spent nine days unconscious in the hospital before he woke up.

To Angela, there had been no question that she would help organize the rescue, regardless of personal difficulty or risk. "On the mountain it is all about teamwork. We look out for each other," Angela emphasizes to other mountaineers and clients. Despite the disruption and very real danger of the rescue, she considered it her duty to give her full effort to save the man. To Angela, that is the unwritten code of an alpinist and a part of the very core of what it means to be a steward of the mountains.

Steadily, Angela continued to earn a solid reputation in the field of mountaineering. Today, as she guides and instructs others, she takes her responsibilities seriously, advocating for safety and for conserving the outdoors. Some of the routes she has climbed or skied in the past are showing real evidence of global warming and are no longer viable. She has also seen the results of people's interactions with the environment. Part of her work today is to campaign for better regulations to protect natural spaces. She is also a business owner. Her company, Chicks Climbing & Skiing, empowers women by training and supporting them in outdoor endeavors.

When asked about her career path and her advice to others, she says, "Follow what makes your heart sing. Don't be constrained by what others think you should do." More than anything, Angela advises others to "look for opportunities to fulfill your curiosity." The more time a person can spend outdoors, the more one's perceptions of the world open up. It is primal, she says. It is what makes us human.

Follow Angela Hawse Online

Website: www.alpinist007.com

Instagram: @alpinist007

Twitter: @alpinist007

Facebook: Angela Hawse

Part V: Adrenaline Earth

Sara Mudallal:
Vault, Leap, Tumble

The camera was rolling as Sara Mudallal poised on the low stone wall. Flexing her knees, she sprang up and pivoted, executing a graceful backflip that landed in a crouch. Leaping from one obstacle to another, her goal was to move quickly and smoothly through each urban feature in her path. Next up was a waist-high railing. Sara ran at it straight on. She gripped the top, planted one foot on the metal, and vaulted over. On the other side now, she twisted her body forward and navigated a narrow ledge that sloped down 45 degrees beside a set of stairs. From there, she jumped over a section of broken concrete and tucked her head in for a careful somersault. She finished up with more jumps and rolls, making the whole sequence look easy—which it wasn't. Not at all.

The video happened when Sara was on a trip to Jordan. Though Sara was born and raised in Los Angeles, her family comes from this country in the Middle East. It was an exciting moment when a representative from Red Bull reached out to Sara while she was in the country visiting her relatives. Would she be interested in participating in a video that would feature her demonstrating her favorite sport, parkour? Yes! Sara scouted the area, identifying interesting obstacles that she knew she could navigate.

"My name is Sara Mudallal," she said as the cameras were rolling. "I'm 23 years old, and I train and practice parkour." She explained that, a few years ago, she began wearing the traditional hijab—headscarf—and practicing parkour at the same time. She elaborated that not many girls were into the sport and especially not in the Arab community. "I hope to see a lot of girls practicing parkour in Jordan one day."

Sara's message is clear, no matter what country she is in. Girls shouldn't be afraid about doing things outside the norm. Whether it's dressing differently or participating in something outside society's expectations, people don't need to change themselves—it's OK to follow an unusual path. "Follow your dream," she says. "Trust me, it will come."

Five-foot-two and with an athletic build, Sara is well equipped for parkour's challenging moves. However, she didn't start practicing the sport until she was 20 years old. Before that, she claims she had a fairly normal childhood. Growing up in sunny Los Angeles meant that she was outside a lot. She was always active, climbing trees and playing basketball and softball for fun, though never on a formal team. She loved to jump on things, to see how she could make her body move. As a child, her favorite movie was *Tarzan*, and perhaps Tarzan's smooth movement through the jungle influenced her to eventually try parkour. In high school she thought she might want to be a veterinarian but changed her mind when she became more interested in her family's shipping business. However, one thing was clear: she definitely didn't want to sit behind a desk all day.

By the time Sara graduated from high school, she had earned her black belt in karate, a discipline she had been studying since she was 12. The hardest part of achieving the black belt status was the commitment, self-control, and patience it took to master it. But she loved that aspect of it, too. Learning how to control her body and how to discipline her mind boosted her self-confidence. The mental and physical strength were enormously helpful when she decided to focus her efforts on parkour.

Sara had recently graduated from college with a bachelor's degree in business marketing when her life took a different turn and parkour came into her life. She and a friend had come across a couple of parkour videos. *Wow*, she thought. *That looks really fun.* Then, when she found out that there was a parkour gym less than ten minutes from her house, she knew she was going to give it a try herself. With a conviction that it was never too late to start something new, she signed up for a class.

Parkour: What Is It?

The word parkour comes from the French term *parcours* and literally means a course or path. The idea of the sport is to move through an environment of obstacles efficiently and smoothly. Parkour athletes use different actions to create a "line," a sequence of jumps, leaps, tumbles, or other movements. Using an environment—usually urban—to create this sequence of moves, a parkour participant is called a *traceuse* (*traceur* for a male). Each traceuse designs her own path forward, navigating over or through obstacles such as walls, railings, and other urban objects. Athletes in the sport embrace a creative interpretation of how to plot a course through a varied landscape.

The act of overcoming obstacles can be transferred to a philosophy held by purists of the sport. Not only does parkour encourage physical self-improvement, but also it inspires a freedom from the constraints of society. By overcoming physical obstacles in one's environment, an athlete can diminish mental blocks and the difficulties of everyday life.

Sara showed up at the Tempest Academy. There were mostly men in the gym and no women wearing hijabs. It didn't matter. Before long, Sara fell in love with parkour. The idea of creatively navigating through an urban environment efficiently and quickly using a variety of moves was fascinating and fun. Starting as an absolute beginner in the sport, she jumped three levels in the first few months. It wasn't easy, though—it took extreme dedication and focus to get things right.

Each new exercise involved a process of learning. Sara remembers how she trained to do a front flip in midair. "When I was 18, I learned how to do a backflip on a trampoline." But when she was a teenager, she could never have imagined doing a tucked flip on an outdoor surface, sometimes over concrete where there was absolutely no room for making a mistake. With the aim of taking the move outside, Sara knew that she would need to get the flip perfect every single time.

To train for the front flip, Sara got back onto the trampoline. The first step was to work on air awareness. She needed to understand exactly where she was in the air, to master control over moving her body where she wanted it to go. Once she was consistently landing the front flip on the trampoline, she moved to a foam pit. There, with plenty of padding to cushion her falls when she didn't make the flip, she practiced, repeating the moves over and over. It needed to be an automatic, nearly unconscious move. Finally, she was ready to try the flip on a floor mat.

Sara stood in the center of the mat. She did one last stretch and then she was ready. Two people stood by to "spot" her. They would guide her body through the movement—and catch her if she messed up. Sara took a few steps to gain momentum, then leaped up, tucked her body, and landed. She'd done it!

It took another four months or so before she could do the flip without help. A year later she took it outside, where she was now able to flip off walls and other obstacles.

Tic Tac to Cat Roll

Parkour is a sport of movement. The creativity of fluidly moving through a landscape is one of its biggest attractions. Because parkour involves a lot of jumping, athletes must first learn how to land. This must be on the balls of the feet and with bent knees to absorb the impact. As soon as a traceuse learns the basics, next comes some of the trickier moves. Tic Tac is when someone uses one surface to push off and gain momentum to leap onto another surface. A cat leap is when someone jumps onto a wall with her hands on top and her feet against the wall's surface. From there, the traceuse pulls herself over. Another move is called a dash vault. In this move, the athlete springs over a low wall or other object, using her hands to propel her away and onto the next obstacle. Whatever the move, parkour athletes learn new moves safely and in progressive steps as they build up their strength, flexibility, and balance.

Today, Sara trains for several hours every day to get better at parkour. Most of the time she follows a schedule. On Mondays and Wednesdays, she works on upper body strength. On Tuesdays, Thursdays, and Saturdays, she focuses on perfecting her moves, things like flips, balancing, and scaling walls. For these, she starts in a gym that is equipped with a trampoline, mats, and plenty of crash pads. She repeats each attempt until the steps are automatic. When she's confident she can pull it off every time, she tries the move outside.

Sara reserves Fridays and Sundays for karate. Her second-degree black belt is in the traditional Japanese martial art called Wadō-ryū (pronounced wa-DOE-roo). In this discipline, the focus is on deflecting moves more than contact with an opponent. Students of this martial arts form learn body awareness techniques and practice fluid movements to avoid impact. Sara's Wadō-ryū training also helps her with parkour.

As Sara's skill improves, she is aware of the lack of other females practicing parkour, though that has never stopped her from training. Initially her parents, though supportive of Sara keeping physically fit, were also skeptical. Parkour was a man's sport, they argued. When was she going to stop practicing?

It was true that many females in Sara's community didn't do sports, and especially not parkour. But, Sara reasoned, that was exactly why she needed to share what she was doing. More than anything, Sara wanted to let others know, especially Muslim girls, that it was OK—fantastic, actually—to partici-pate in sports and follow your passion. She wrote down her goals and posted them on a vision board in her room: "Get sponsored by Adidas," "Meet people and create communities," "Travel the world." She reasoned that if her goals were written down and in front of her, she would keep thinking about them and work toward the things that mattered to her.

The Path of the Warrior

George Herbert was a French naval officer who helped evacuate hundreds of people after a devastating volcanic eruption in the Caribbean. After watching how the indigenous peoples made their way easily through the altered landscape while those of European descent struggled with each new obstacle, George became obsessed with movement, particularly efficient movement. He eventually created a fitness regimen he called "The Natural Method." Later, all French military units adopted the training, building strength and character through running obstacle courses which they called *parcours du combatant*, or the path of the warrior.

David Belle is considered the founder of parkour as we know it today. His father, having trained in the French military, taught him the basics of the discipline. David took it from there, forming a team of traceurs they called the Yamikazi and gaining recognition for his work. In 2008, the World Freerunning Parkour Federation opened its doors and introduced the world to the sport of parkour.

As Sara posted more of her videos online, people began to take notice. It was clear that she was doing something special.

One day a reporter from Fox News in Los Angeles asked Sara if they could do a story on her. The result was a two-minute segment on the morning news highlighting Sara's commitment to the sport. When the reporter asked her to elaborate on the dangers of the moves she was performing, Sara had an easy answer: "Once you hit that fear in the face, knock it out of the way, you just feel that excitement and rush." Perhaps even more impressive than Sara's ability to overcome her fear to do the challenging moves was her ability to do something she loved, despite being female—and Muslim. "My message is to inspire women to do what they love no matter what they wear, whether its religion, culture, personal preference. . . I want them to do it with love and confidence." The segment dubbed Sara a "Fearless Female."

Soon Sara received more recognition. This time a producer from Hollywood reached out. "I like your Instagram. Have you ever thought of applying for *American Ninja Warrior*?"

"Well, I am now."

Sara had watched the popular TV program but had never considered applying. But as she watched old episodes of competitors attempting to complete the show's obstacle course, she was intrigued. She knew she was in great physical shape. Her parkour moves were better than ever. Maybe she *could* compete . . .

Sara put together a demo video and filled out the application, including several pages of questions such as "What three words would your friends use to describe you?" and "Do people ever underestimate you?" Since the obstacle course would be built over a pool of water, another question asked, "Do you swim?"

When Sara got the call that she had been accepted as a contestant, she made history. She would be the first woman ever to wear a hijab on the program.

Compete Like a Ninja

The TV program *American Ninja Warrior* premiered in 2009, a spin-off from the similar Japanese production called *Sasuke*. In the series, contestants who successfully navigate a challenging obstacle course earn a cash prize. While over 70,000 people apply each year, only 100 are invited onto the show, and 30 percent of those are previous participants. The application process is lengthy. It includes several pages of questions along with a mandatory two- to three-minute demonstration video. In addition to those chosen ahead of time, there is a last-minute walk-on process where anyone present can enter their name into a random drawing of additional contestants. The event starts with qualifying rounds. Only those competitors who make it farthest in the course in the quickest amount of time go on to the national finals, held each year in Las Vegas. Here there is a one-million-dollar cash prize for contestants who complete all four stages of the extreme obstacle course.

Sara participated in the tenth season of *American Ninja Warrior* wearing a shirt that proclaimed, "Change Nothing." Several friends and family members came to watch, their T-shirts proudly displaying a "Team Sara" logo. It was March, and though not exactly cold, the event was filmed after dark and it was chilly. There was special theme that night. It was "Jurassic World Night" in celebration of the upcoming movie *Jurassic World: Fallen Kingdom.* The dinosaur costumes and decorations added to the excitement. When Sara arrived, an escort brought her to the back lot of Universal Studios where the contest was set up. The course—with the water pits under each obstacle— gleamed under the lights. It looked . . . challenging.

None of the contestants were allowed a practice round on the course. Sara would have one shot only at each of the six obstacles. She listened carefully as a crew member described each feature, giving advice about the best way to progress. Could she do this?

Finally, it was Sara's turn. She paused at the entrance to the course. The first section, called "floating steps," consisted of five angled pads that she would have to leap onto one by one before grabbing a rope to swing to the first platform. Go! Speed was the key to success. Sara clambered onto the first pad, then jumped to the next. She grabbed the rope, aiming for the platform, slipped, but saved herself. She made it to the first platform! Next up was the jumper cable section.

Two grips hung from chains over the second pool of water. To successfully negotiate this section, Sara would need to hang onto the grips and swing to a giant punching bag, which would propel her to the next safety platform. She jumped, clasping the grips but not gaining enough momentum to make it to the bag. *Why aren't I swinging farther?* she asked herself. She dropped into the cold pool below. Shivering, she stepped off the set, disappointed that she was now disqualified, but proud to have gotten as far as she did. Months later when the episode was aired on TV, there was a clip of Sara's attempt. "I'm actually featured on TV, on *American Ninja Warrior*! Holy cow!"

The American Ninja experience wasn't Sara's last time on TV. Next she landed a part in a CarMax commercial. The commercial's theme was "If you're going to put a sticker on your car, it has to mean something." Sara was thrilled to include her bumper sticker: "J'adore Parkour." *Yes*, she thought as she drove her truck in the commercial, *I really do love parkour.*

Another gig involved participating in a music video. It was for Bebe Rexha's official "You Can't Stop the Girl" video. One scene shows Sara running with Bebe in an expression of solidarity. Later in the sequence, she demonstrated a smooth vault over a bark bench. As Sara takes on more challenges and perfects her skill in parkour, the words of Bebe's song echo throughout her life:

You can't stop the girl from going.
You can't stop the world from knowing.
The truth will set you free.
You can't stop the girl . . .

Follow Sara Mudallal Online

Instagram: @saramudallal

Twitter: @sara_mudallal

Facebook: Sara Mudallal

YouTube channel: Sara Mudallal

14

Brittany Leavitt:
Teacher Turned Climber

The rock face was nearly vertical. The surface was an uneven expanse of cracks, protrusions, and jagged edges of mica schist, a compact type of rock that would not crumble or break. Because of the large, protruding section about halfway up the wall's surface, the climbing community referred to this formation as "The Bulge." Today, Brittany Leavitt would be climbing a straight route to the top. Because of the overhang, she would not be able to see her feet as she climbed past it. Instead, wearing a harness attached to a belay rope, Brittany would navigate this section of the rock by feel. The rope was there for safety, so that if she did lose her grip, it would catch her before she plummeted to the ground. But she wouldn't let that happen. Today Brittany planned to use her own strength and skill to propel herself all the way to the top.

The Bulge is located in Hades Heights, a series of rock formations in Carderock, Maryland. Popular with the local climbing community, the Bulge is a top-rope climb—this means that the safety rope is anchored from the top. A person at the bottom gathers the rope as a climber gets higher, ensuring the rope remains taut in case of a fall.

Making the Grade

With a difficulty rating of 5.10, the Bulge is no beginner's task. Climbers use a system of measurement to assess the difficulty of a particular climb. The Yosemite Decimal System (YDS) identifies five route classifications. Class one means the route is flat and easily hiked, while class five refers to vertical terrain where a safety rope is necessary. Under class five are sub-categories ranging from 5.1 to 6.0. The lower the number, the easier the climb. For example, a 5.1 to 5.4 face has plenty of large handholds and footholds. Beyond a 5.12 rating, the climb is considered experts-only. A 6.0 is a sheer rock face, impossible to climb without using aids—bolts or devices placed in the rock to help the ascent. There is also a system for suggested time necessary for the climb. Grade I means that you should be at the top in an hour or two, but Grade VI refers to an excursion of two or more days.

Though she was an experienced rock climber, Brittany felt a pulse of excitement as she pulled on her climbing shoes and snugged the Velcro ties across the top of her bare feet (no socks helped ensure the best foot grip). She checked the knot securing the rope to the harness resting on her hips. With a glance at the vertical task above her, she dipped her hand into the bag of chalk—a fine powder made from magnesium carbonate—attached to her back. The powder absorbed moisture and would help prevent her fingers from slipping. With the limited handholds and footholds she would use to traverse the rock face, she needed total control.

Then, Brittany was on the wall. One reach at a time, she inched her way up. When she got to the bulge, she hesitated. For a moment she had forgotten to put both hands above her and her body was in an awkward position. She moved her left arm to get a purchase on the uneven rock. She felt below for the next viable grip with her foot. Blind, she found it and moved another step up. Then another. There was no room for fear. Instead, adrenaline, passion, and courage surged through her—it would take all three to make it to the top.

When she finally crested the lip of the rock face, Brittany broke into a giant grin. This was what she was meant to do.

Brittany was adopted into a multiracial family of six brothers and sisters. She is the youngest daughter. As a child she was often the quiet one, but also the one who was always taking risks, pushing herself to do more than her siblings. From the moment she could walk, she loved to be outdoors. Her family nicknamed her the "barefoot kid" because whenever she could, she opted to forgo shoes so she could feel the grass and dirt between her toes. A born naturalist, she spent her childhood collecting worms and insects, fishing with her family, or lying on a picnic blanket outside, immersed in a favorite book. She also took equestrian lessons for ten years, savoring the chance to experience the outdoors from the back of a horse.

The first time she tried climbing, Brittany was at an indoor facility with friends from college. As the people around her discussed the best way to climb the wall, she didn't understand half of what they were saying. This was a whole new language and experience. And it was daunting. How could she navigate all those narrow holds to get to the top of the wall? Still, Brittany was game to try. She climbed up the wall haphazardly, not following a particular route, but just trying to get as high as she could. Brittany later learned that what she was doing was called "rainbowing." Different routes were color coordinated. She gripped whatever holds were closest and easiest without trying to follow a particular one-color route. Despite not knowing what she was doing, Brittany was intrigued. After coming back several times to try again, it didn't take long for her to want to take the sport outdoors.

Using hand-me-down equipment and learning as much as she could, Brittany began climbing outdoors. She found like-minded people and joined organizations such as Brown Girls Climb and Outdoor Afro. Both groups emphasized acquiring skills while building a community. The organizations and people were exactly what Brittany was looking for.

As the regional local leader coordinator for Brown Girls Climb, Brittany soon got involved in a festival called Color the

Crag. At the event, she helped organize an inclusive gathering of outdoor enthusiasts who met to "celebrate diversity in the sport of rock climbing." Over the four-day weekend, participants had the opportunity to attend various workshops, including some on different types of climbing, injury prevention, and even backpack cooking. Located an hour north of Birmingham, Alabama, a privately owned nature park called Horse Pens 40 (HP40) was the perfect venue for the festival. By now Brittany was an accomplished climber and an instructor for REI (Recreational Equipment Inc. is a company specializing in outdoor clothing and gear). For the Color the Crag event, Brittany was appointed director of operations. Passionate about the sport, she was thrilled to introduce others, especially those who had traditionally been underrepresented, to the world of climbing.

Bouldering and Beyond

Climbs are classified by the height and equipment used. The greatest risk is with free soloing, where climbers don't use ropes, instead climbing entirely without aid. Bouldering doesn't involve ropes, either, but the distance to the ground is under 20 feet (6 m). With just a couple of crash pads at the bottom in case something does go wrong, bouldering requires strength along with technical skill and concentration. Climbers work on difficult moves, called problems, as they navigate a rock face. Next is free-climbing, which is broken into two subgroups: traditional "trad" climbing and sport climbing. Both use ropes, a harness, and a belay partner—someone who will pay out the rope as the climber ascends. In trad climbing, removable hardware is placed in cracks and crevices to make a rock face easier to climb. This is called protection or simply "pro." In sport climbing, permanent bolts in the rock help map out the route for each section or pitch of the climb. In addition, athletes can sometimes use a webbed ladder called an etrier or other devices for the more difficult sections of a rock face.

One day, Brittany was on her way to lead an Outdoor Afro event in Baltimore. Outdoor Afro involves a "cutting edge network that celebrates and inspires African American connections and leadership in nature." She had been a leader of the organization for a while and loved the chance to meet up with others to enjoy the outdoors. She was just about to walk out the door to head to the event when she paused to check her email one more time. "Congratulations!" the email began. She was in! Several weeks earlier, Brittany had put her name on a list of those interested in completing a climb on Mount Kilimanjaro in Tanzania. Never expecting to be chosen, Brittany reread the email. It was true! She had been chosen to join a team of 11 members from Outdoor Afro on an expedition to climb Africa's highest mountain. Brittany's team would be the second African American group ever to attempt the climb.

Brittany sat down to think about the expedition. It would be the farthest she had ever traveled and perhaps the most adventurous thing she had attempted. The first thing she did was celebrate. The next thing she did was come up with a training schedule.

But how do you prepare for an ascent so high that the air becomes thin and even walking can become a challenge? she wondered. With her full-time job as an early childhood educator for the Smithsonian Institution in Washington, DC, Brittany knew that taking time off to hike comparable mountains in the United States was out of the question. She decided to strengthen her muscles—and especially her lungs—through running and weight lifting. With under a year to train, there was no time to waste.

Kilimanjaro

Mount Kilimanjaro is the highest free standing mountain in the world and part of the Seven Summits challenge, the highest peaks on each of the earth's continents. Located in Tanzania, this stratovolcano's highest point is Uhuru Peak, towering 19,340 feet (5,895 m) above sea level. Though there had been many previous attempts, the first recorded summit occurred in 1889. Sheila Mac-Donald earned credit for the first female ascent in 1927. Recently, Anne Lorimor set a record for the oldest person to successfully summit. She was 89 years old.

Not everyone who tries reaches the top of Kilimanjaro. Failure to summit is mostly due to severe weather or altitude sickness. The extreme height of the peak means that air pressure—and the ability to intake enough oxygen—is much less than in lower climes. Without enough oxygen entering the lungs, people can become critically ill and even die if they don't resolve the issue quickly.

Finally, it was time. Brittany flew to Kilimanjaro Airport where she met with the rest of the Outdoor Afro expedition team. She had already seen the mountain from the plane, a majestic fortress resting under an intense sun. Brittany was awed. As she walked through the small airport, she told herself, "I'm back home and into a land that was meant for me to connect to."

Now it was time for final preparations. With several choices of routes to the top, Brittany's team had opted for the Machame Route, a trek that would take them seven days. The night before at the hotel in Arusha was an exciting one. One after another, questions raced through Brittany's head: *What will it be like to camp on the mountain? How cold and how hot will it be? What will we be eating? Did I bring the right clothing and gear? Will we see monkeys? What about altitude sickness—will I experience it and how dangerous is it?*

Brittany assembled and reassembled the 32-pound (14.5-kg) day pack she would be carrying with her. The expedition porters would carry one further duffel bag per person.

Brittany's was stuffed with her sleeping bag, extra clothes, and the gear she didn't need with her every day. The porters would also haul up tents, sleeping mats, and plenty of extra water.

Finally, the night before the expedition, Brittany tried to sleep. The instructions of the guides played in her mind. Over and over they had reminded the group to take it slowly. It was the only way to acclimate to less oxygen and to avoid getting sick. *Polepole* (pronounced PAH-ley-PAH-ley) was Swahili for "slowly," and the guides repeated the instruction again and again.

The next day was beautiful. The team had lucked out with no rain. Suddenly, they were at the entrance to Kilimanjaro National Park and the expedition was starting. They walked through a lush, green rain forest. (There were monkeys!) Also called the Cloud Forest, it was a misty, magical place. Outdoor Afro had provided the team with excellent hiking boots. Brittany was glad of them as she walked along the muddy path. That first day they gained only about 3.5 miles (5.6 km) but ascended nearly 4,000 feet (1,220 m). *Polepole*, Brittany told herself.

Machame Camp at night was spectacular. Brittany couldn't remember the last time she had seen the Milky Way in such a clear, dazzling way. She felt, more than ever, that she needed to encourage others to experience the out-of-doors, too. As an REI instructor, she often met people who had never camped or set foot in the wilderness. She vowed to share her experience so she could inspire others to move past their comfort zones, maybe not something as radical as trekking Kilimanjaro, but definitely experiencing nature.

Brittany's team hiked farther up the mountain each day, through four different temperate zones. Some sections of the trek were barren of any vegetation, and the higher they got to the summit, the colder and windier it got, too, sometimes dipping as low as 28 degrees Fahrenheit (–2°C) at night. During the middle of the day it could warm up to 40 or 50 degrees.

Except for the summit attempt, the schedule for each day involved getting up at 6:30 AM and setting out around 8:00. Each day included a five- to seven-hour hike. The elevation steadily increased. With it was the potential for altitude sickness, a condition that would end up costing Brittany the summit—but potentially saving her life.

Thin Air

While there are no technically difficult sections on Kilimanjaro requiring ropes or specialized equipment, there is only about a 66 percent chance of reaching Uhuru Summit from the Machame Route. This is mostly due to the body's reaction to the decreased air pressure so high up. Anything over 26,000 feet (7,920 m) is considered the "death zone," and humans cannot survive more than a few hours at this height. While Kilimanjaro's summit is 19,341 feet (5,895 m), it is still considered an extreme altitude.

Acute Mountain Sickness (AMS) is the mildest form of thin

air sickness. The symptoms include headaches and nausea. As it gets worse, a person might experience shortness of breath, mental confusion, and vomiting. HAPE and HACE are two altitude-induced conditions even more serious. In these ailments, fluid builds up either in the lungs or in the brain, leading to death in less than 24 hours if left to continue.

Brittany and her team were at approximately 17,000 feet (5,180 m). Already, two members of the expedition had aborted due to dehydration and altitude sickness issues. The temperature was intense. Despite her layers, Brittany's hands felt like they were freezing, and she could barely grip her trekking poles. *I can't stop now,* she told herself. It was dark, too. They had started their push to the summit at 11:00 PM the previous night in order to reach the peak and then descend safely as quickly as possible. The darkness would last until they reached Stella Point at 18,871 feet (5,752 m). The total time to Uhuru Peak was approximately ten hours. From the summit back down to a safer elevation would take another six hours. The last day was brutal.

Still in the dark, Brittany focused on the headlamp of the guide ahead of her. *I just need to power through this.* An intense wind howled as she concentrated on moving forward. The guides stopped the group. "We can see snow," one of them said. That meant that Stella Point was close. "Yup," Brittany responded with her addled brain, a symptom, she realized later, of AMS. She turned to a teammate. "I need to sit down."

The next moments were a blur. Somehow, Brittany had passed out. When she came to, the guides gently told her that she needed to go back.

Though initially devastated, Brittany knew that no mountain was worth risking injury—or worse. No matter where she was in nature—on Kilimanjaro or bouldering near her hometown of Baltimore, Maryland—Brittany knew that the number one consideration was always safety. As she made her way down the mountain, she reflected on all the novice climbers she had encountered throughout her various leadership roles. Many times, they had let fear stop them from even beginning something new. In this case, she had done an incredible thing, pushing herself to her limit, but also recognizing when it was time to stop. Getting to the summit was only a few hours. What she had learned about herself would last her lifetime.

Back in the United States, Brittany continued to seek out more and more leadership roles. One of her favorite things to do was to help others in the sport, teaching individuals as well as classes. To her, climbing was more than a sport—it was a way to connect to others. It was never about being number one or about conquering a mountain or crag. It was about building confidence and pushing past her mental barriers to accomplish things she didn't think possible—like she had with the Kilimanjaro trip. Brittany considers the outdoors an excellent teacher, and now she works to share what she has learned, inflaming the feeling of accomplishment in others.

"You don't have to change yourself to be part of this culture. You don't have to be someone wearing the fancy stuff or someone with all the gear. Just go out and don't second-guess yourself."

For Brittany, her connection to the outdoors is a fundamental part of who she is. Sharing this love with others is essential. Today you will find Brittany wherever there's a rock face to explore and a community to share it with.

Follow Brittany Leavitt Online

Website: www.britleavitt.com

Instagram: @bleavitt8

Twitter: @bleavitt8

Facebook: Brittany Leavitt

Courtney Dauwalter:
Up and Running

Hours: 100

Miles: 205.5 (330 km)

Elevation gain: 40,200 feet (12,250 m)

All you have to do is move yourself with your feet across beautiful trails, Courtney Dauwalter coached herself as she thought about the race she was about to enter. She helped herself to more coffee. It was 6:00 in the morning. In just three hours she would join 249 others for the Tahoe 200 Ultra Endurance Run. While the race stipulated that runners had a maximum of 100 hours to complete the circuit, Courtney's goal was to finish in half that time. She aimed to beat the old record of 58 hours and 29 minutes. To do so she would have to run night and day for the next two days, pausing only briefly at various aid stations set up along the route. The course included steep hills and single-track trails with only about 30 miles (48 km) of running on mostly unpaved roads. There was a ton that could go wrong, but Courtney knew she could do it—at least she hoped so.

Courtney sat down to smear lubricant between her toes to guard against chafing and blisters for the next 50 hours. She pulled on toe socks. Separating her toes would help to keep them from rubbing against each other, too. She had on loose clothing—comfortable long shorts and a roomy T-shirt. She planned to put on a light jacket when the sun—and temperature—went down, but otherwise, these would be the clothes she would wear for the next 200 miles. All she needed now was her running vest and she was ready to go. She couldn't wait!

At 9:00 AM, Courtney stood at the starting gate at Homewood Ski Resort, just south of Tahoe City, California. Since the race followed the Tahoe Rim Trail around the lake, this would be the finish line as well. It was hot and there was no wind, but that didn't bother Courtney. She had run in all sorts of conditions before. The other runners jostled around her as the race official counted down. They were off! It didn't take Courtney long to pull in front.

The initial aid station came quickly—Courtney arrived 25 minutes before her crew expected her. This team consisted of her dad, her husband, a training partner, and a pacer who would run beside her for short periods of the run. For now, Courtney was ahead of the rest of the runners, but there was a problem. Her stomach was upset, and it was hard to eat anything without throwing it back up. It didn't stop her, however—Courtney knew how to push through discomfort. With a quick hug for each of her crew, she was off.

At 50 miles (80 km), Courtney was still at the front of the pack. At mile 65 (105 km), she was nearly an hour and a half ahead of her closest competitor, Kyle Curtin. She increased that time by another 30 minutes at mile 102 (165 km). She ran through the night, but by early the next morning, she admitted that things weren't going well at all. Normally there would be points when she felt great followed by expected periods of feeling low. Now it seemed like she was fighting for every mile. Plus, every time she came to an aid station, she sat down while her crew gave her food—ramen noodles, pancakes, quesadillas, mashed potatoes. She ate whatever she felt like eating, but her stomach was still not cooperating. She kept going.

At 3:59 AM the next morning, she was only eight minutes ahead of Kyle. At mile 181 (290 km), she had been running for over 42 hours. The constant pounding and lack of adequate food or sleep was taking a toll on her. When Kyle passed her, she wasn't surprised. But, with less than a marathon distance to go, she now had another goal. She very much wanted to finish the race in under 50 hours. It was going to be tight.

Courtney passed the finish line at 10:44 AM with a time of 49 hours, 54 minutes, and 35 seconds. She finished second overall after Kyle, but first among the women. Not only that— Courtney had beaten the Tahoe 200 Ultra's old record by over *eight and a half hours*! She sat down to celebrate—and change her shoes.

Courtney grew up in Minnesota, the only girl in a family of five. "I was in every sport possible," she reflected. "There were always multiple things going on." The family had one rule, however: Courtney and her brothers needed to finish whatever they started. For example, the year Courtney took up softball, she played out the season even though she knew it wasn't the sport for her. What she did enjoy was Nordic skiing—and running. In high school she was a state champion in Nordic skiing and consequently earned an athletic scholarship to the University of Denver in Colorado. Initially she wasn't sure what profession to study: Writer? Scientist? Astronaut? A position in sports medicine? Finally, she set her sights on teaching, taking a job as a science teacher in Mississippi when she graduated. The only problem was that Mississippi didn't have snow. Nordic skiing was out. What could she do instead?

Courtney had always been a runner. Alongside the skiing, she had participated in track and field in high school. Now she signed up for a marathon. It was scary to stand at the starting line, though, wondering if she could last for the entire 26.2-mile race. She reminded herself that she loved running. It was a sport where she was in control, the steering wheel for her own success. By the end of the marathon, Courtney was surprised she had made it but exhilarated, too. She felt like she could keep going, maybe not forever, but definitely farther. What if she tried it? How would it be to push herself even more? Courtney decided to find out.

More than a Marathon

A marathon is 26.2 miles long (42.1 km) and takes the average person about four and a half hours, more or less, to complete. An ultra is anything more than a marathon and is measured either by distance run or time lapsed. For example, some ultra races are 50, 100, or 200 miles long (80, 160, or 320 km). Aside from the longer distance, these contests may include other challenges such as weather or terrain. The Western States 100 includes both snow and excessive heat depending on the altitude at various points on the rugged trails in the Sierra Nevada mountains of California. Worldwide, ultras offer different tests. The temperature during the Marathon des Sables in Morocco can reach 120 degrees Fahrenheit (49°C) and the six-day staged race requires runners to carry all their supplies except water. In Peru, the Jungle Ultra takes runners through a rain forest where there is 100 percent humidity. Ultras that are based on time give contestants a certain number of hours to complete a distance. In 24-hour races, contestants run as far as they can in one full day.

The Prickly Pear Race in San Antonio, Texas, was a different kind of race than anything Courtney had tried before. Measured in kilometers, the 50 kilometers (31 miles) was only a few miles longer than a marathon. But instead of on a road or sidewalk, the route wound along a single track through the woods. The first section was a loop of 5 kilometers (3.1 miles) followed by three loops of 15 kilometers (9.32 miles) each. Starting at 7:00 in the morning, runners had a cutoff time of 3:00 that afternoon. Another fun feature was that the trail was broken up by aid stations. There, runners could help themselves to water and food treats—Courtney stocked up on a handful of jelly beans.

Running the extra distance turned out to be no problem, and Courtney earned a first-place finish at the Prickly Pear. So, what about going farther still? This time she signed up for the Run Rabbit Run 50-miler in Colorado. Unlike San Antonio, where heat was a major contender, here it was the intense cold that contributed to the challenge. At points along the trail it snowed, hailed, and poured down rain. Despite this, the contestants were ecstatic, thrilled to be running and competing together in such an empowering atmosphere. For Courtney, finishing that many miles using nothing but foot power, hooked her like nothing before. Next up, 100 miles.

After pressing herself to run longer and longer distances, it seemed like Courtney couldn't be stopped. The next year, when she competed in the Run Rabbit Run 100, Courtney was forced to recalibrate those expectations. It reminded her that failure can happen, but that it's often the best incentive for succeeding the next time.

To run 100 miles (160 km), you need mental muscle as well as physical strength. When Courtney was in high school, she had a coach who trained her team to acknowledge their "pain cave" and to work through it. The sustained effort of running mile after mile puts enormous strain on the body. For example, it is critical to stay hydrated and to take in enough calories to maintain the energy needed to continue. Courtney was doing those things, but for the Run Rabbit Run 100, when the tough part came and her body wanted to stop, she focused on the discomfort instead of when she would get through it. For the first time in a long time, Courtney quit something she started, earning a DNF (did not finish) for the race.

Afterward, the decision to quit that race gnawed at her. It had seemed impossible to keep running at the time, but the more she thought about it, the more Courtney questioned that choice. *I have to try again*, she told herself. *I will try again.* This time, though, she would work up to it. She would be better prepared.

A Run Through History

Throughout history, the idea of running for miles or even days is nothing new, whether to stalk prey or deliver messages—or for sport. Officially, the first Olympic marathon took place in 1896, followed the next year by today's oldest annual 26.2-miler, the Boston Marathon (initially the American Marathon). Fast forward to the 20th century, when footraces grew in popularity until contests longer than a marathon were popping up all over. Ted Corbitt, founder of the Road Runners Club of America, coined the term "ultrarunning" in the 1970s to label these longer competitions. In May 1981, *Ultrarunning Magazine* opened its doors and provided a central publication to cater to the burgeoning sport. Next, the International Association of Ultrarunning (IAU), the governing organization for world championships, regulations, and records, was founded in 1984. Today, the IAU estimates that the number of ultrarunners has increased by over 300 percent in the past ten years.

Two weeks after the Run Rabbit Run 100, Courtney entered a 31-mile (50-km) race. She came in 30th place. It was a respectable finish, but she knew she could do better. Four and a half months later she entered—and won—a 50-mile race, finishing in 8 hours, 17 minutes, and 4 seconds. She raised the bar higher, next running a 52.4-miler (84.3 km). When she earned third place, she knew she was ready to attempt an even greater distance.

The FANS 24-Hour Race was appealing to Courtney for many reasons. First, there was no pressure to complete a set number of miles. The race was timed instead. Her result would be based on how many miles she could complete in 24 hours. The race took place in Courtney's home state of Minnesota. The course itself was mostly flat, consisting of loops rather than one continuous circuit. Another plus was that the event's proceeds went to charity.

Despite the level terrain, the day—and night—was going to be extreme. Courtney's goal was to run 100 miles (160 km), but she also told herself that just to finish was going to be a success. It would be exhausting to go without sleep and to sustain exercise for that long. Race officials knew how challenging and dangerous it could be, too. The race included mandatory weight checks every four hours. If anyone dropped more than 5 percent of their prerace weight, they had to rest and rejuvenate with water and food until they put the weight back on. *Just keep going and do your best*, Courtney told herself. She would do what she could in 24 hours and see what happened.

Courtney ran. Whenever her body wanted to quit, she pushed through it, recognizing that this was part of the process. The race allowed outsiders to run with the contestants for short periods, so it was wonderful when family members along with Courtney's old neighbors and even her high school coach came to run a few miles with her. She was elated when she clocked 100 miles—but then crushed to learn that she still had three hours to go before the 24 hours were up. When the race finally ended, she had put in 105.05 miles (169.06 km) and finished in second place! Now it was time to see what else she could do.

That year Courtney entered three more races, including another 100-miler, where she came in second again. Her participation accelerated over the next few years. When she came back to the FANS 24-Hour Race the following year, she ran for 123.6 miles (198.9 km)—and this time she came in first.

Courtney traveled all over the country, racking up podium finishes. No longer teaching at this point, her focus was on training herself to go farther than ever. She loved it! When Courtney ran over 155 miles (89 km) in the next 24-hour race she entered, she broke the record for American women. Suddenly, interviews and publicity were taking up nearly as much time as the actual races, it seemed. Courtney had always wanted to travel. Now she had her chance, entering races in France, Ireland, Taiwan, Japan, Canada, and Portugal. It was during the Taiwan 24-hour Ultra that Courtney beat her own record. This time she ran an astonishing 158.97 miles (255.94 km). Later, in an untimed endurance contest called the Big Backyard Ultra, she ran for 279 miles (449 km) over two and a half days.

Last Woman Standing: Maggie Guterl

The Big Backyard Ultra in Bell Buckle, Tennessee, doesn't rely on a set distance or time. Instead, participants compete until every person except one drops out. Dubbed a "last man standing" race, each year, participants line up at the starting gate at 6:35 AM on the first day of the race and run a circuit of approximately 4.16 miles (6.69 km) once every hour.

In 2019 Maggie Guterl was the first woman ever to win this contest, averaging a 54-minute loop each hour for 60 total hours. In the six minutes of down time between each loop, Maggie rested, ate (perogies and noodles, among other things), and prepared to run again. She continued, day and night, until there were eight, then three, then two people left: her and Will Hayward. The two continued the race for another eight hours. During Maggie's last loop, she ran through darkness and rain with five minutes to spare before the starting whistle for the next loop. Will wasn't there; since he failed to make it back in time, Maggie secured the win. She had run 250 miles (402 km), beating her previous best of 183.334 miles (295 km) the year before.

What's her secret for success? Maggie shared that it's a lot of positive self-talk. "Don't think about it. Stay in the moment. Give it everything with an honest effort."

Depending on the kind of run, Courtney prepares for each a little differently. Every time, however, she wears a running hydration vest. This snug-fitting garment allows her to carry essentials she might need along the route. She brings food and usually one to two liters of water to keep her going. Also in her vest are things like ChapStick, tissues, and a hat and gloves, depending on the weather. Although she sometimes listens to music, Courtney mostly prefers the sounds of nature. During training, she practices placing supply items in various compartments of her vest to make sure nothing flops around while she's distance running. For some races where the aid stations might be up to twenty miles apart, it's critical to bring extra nourishment and supplies. Along with food tailored for endurance athletes, she will often bring mashed potatoes, prepacked into reusable baby food pouches. This provides her with the staying power to keep going.

Each ultrarunning event has unique challenges. Sometimes the trouble comes from outside sources such as bad weather, intense hot or cold temperatures, or difficult terrain. Some races wind along uneven trails or include tricky sections including up and down steep hills. Sometimes it's a mental obstacle, like when lack of sleep or extreme fatigue makes Courtney want to stop. That's when experience kicks in to help. Courtney says it's like she has a filing cabinet in her brain. As she completes more races, she can tap into her prior challenges. *You've been here before*, she reminds herself. *You can keep pushing*. With every race Courtney wonders, *What are the limits to the human body? What are* my *limits?*

There have been other circumstances to test Courtney as well. One challenge is hallucinations. Common in ultrarunning, seeing things that aren't there has a scientific explanation. When the brain processes the world around us, data from the optic nerve travels to the brain for interpretation. Lack of sleep and low body fuel can trigger flawed images—sometimes highly imaginative and bizarre.

When Courtney first experienced this phenomenon, it was scary. She perceived giraffes next to the trail and flying eels that made her duck. None of it was real. Now, knowing that hallucinations may happen, Courtney is much calmer when she sees something out of the ordinary, such as a colonial woman churning butter, a leopard in a hammock, or dozens of white cats strolling along the trail.

Today, Courtney is a full-time ultrarunner with no plans to slow down anytime soon. Whether she's running along a solitary, peaceful mountain trail, repeating a loop for 24 hours, or competing for Team USA, Courtney keeps putting one foot in front of the other. Who knows where her two feet will take her next? One thing is for certain; wherever life takes her, Courtney will keep running—strong, free, and connected.

Follow Courtney Dauwalter Online

Instagram: @courtneydauwalter

Twitter: @courtdauwalter

Facebook: Courtney Dauwalter

Afterword

Seek Your Thrill

Excited? Pumped up? Ready to take action? While the women in this book are at the top of their game, they were once beginners, perhaps like some of you. Their first step—and it can be yours, too—was to find their passion, that thing they couldn't stop thinking about and that they really want to pursue. Take a moment to answer these questions: What kind of person are you? What do you enjoy?

If you love getting a bird's-eye view of the world, for example, maybe someday you'd like to try wingsuit flying or skydiving like Roberta Mancino or Melanie Curtis. If you wish you could conquer your fear and increase your ability to focus *no matter what*, highlining like Faith Dickey might be your thing. Or perhaps you're obsessed with speed. If so, you could take Sneha Sharma's lead and power around a racetrack in a Formula car or, like Elladee Brown, launch your mountain bike down a beautiful wilderness trail.

Still unsure? Ask yourself this: Are you an explorer? An adventurer? Someone who likes to push the limits and try new things? Are you curious? To get started in an action sport, you have to start at the beginning. Although there are many ways to do that, each one of the women in this book followed a sequence of steps. They pinpointed a goal. They studied how others did it and asked questions. They found somewhere to practice and then kept at it again and again until they got it right. Sometimes they failed, but they were resilient.

Maybe you're wondering where to go to try an action sport for the first time. After a couple YouTube videos sparked Sara Mudallal's interest, she located a parkour gym near her house and booked a session. Brittany Leavitt tried out the climbing wall in a gym before getting hooked on rock climbing outdoors. When Ann Marie Stephens got home from a snorkeling trip, she looked up the closest dive shop that offered scuba lessons. It doesn't have to cost a lot of money, either. Lizzie Armanto started on an inexpensive skateboard from her neighborhood toy store.

Are you convinced? If not, think about Brittany Hamilton who paddled into the waves with a surfboard and only one arm— just to see if she could do it. Consider Courtney Dauwalter who simply started running and kept pushing herself to see how far she could go. Or, reflect on when Julia Marino broke her skis, and she chose to give snowboarding a shot rather than quitting for the day. Action athletes seek out opportunities.

The bottom line is that you never know what you'll love until you try it. Sure, it might take some research, and it might even be a little scary. Take a breath and start slowly. Everyone does! But once you find your passion, don't let anything get in the way of pursuing it. With a go-for-it attitude, the ocean, track, snow, earth, or sky is the limit!

Acknowledgments

This is a book about people. Amazing, stunning, vibrantly alive people. When I set out to compile the stories of these inspirational go-getters, little did I know that I'd be connecting with people all over from world, traveling (virtually) from India to Italy, from Alaska to the Antarctic. My sincere gratitude goes first to the women in this book, each a humble and generous person who opened up in a way that made me catch a glimpse of lives lived to the maximum. I appreciate, too, those who helped me research and understand this pursuit of something meaningful, people like wing walker Marilyn Mason, flying trapeze artist Rebecca Miller, rock- and ice-climber Prerna Dangi, and so many others.

Speaking of rocks, I am especially grateful to my rock-star agent, James McGowan, who is smart and dedicated and makes me laugh. He made the whole process understandable—and fun! Truly, thank you. Of course, editor extraordinaire Jerome Pohlen deserves a giant shout out as well. This is our second book together, and once again his savvy guidance and keen insight made this book better than I could have ever done on my own. Thank you, Jerry.

Writing a book involves a ton of behind-the-scenes support as well. How lucky am I to have such a fantastic critique group? Thank you to Laura Gehl, Hena Khan, and Joan Waites. You are the best! With gratitude and love, I appreciate my family's support. Thanks, Mom and Dad! Thank you, husband and best friend Rich! Hugs to my cheerleader kids!

Finally, for those I haven't specifically named here, understand that I appreciate you more than I know how to write.

Notes

Chapter 1: Roberta Mancino
"Don't fly too close": All quotes from original author interview with Roberta Mancino on December 17, 2019.

Chapter 2: Faith Dickey
"That's impossible": "A Free Solo Examination, Part Two," *MtnMeister* accessed September 14, 2020, http://mtnmeister.com/meister/faith-dickey/.

Oh man, if I don't: All quotes from original author interview with Faith Dickey on October 21, 2019, unless otherwise noted here.

Am I safe?: "Deciphering Fear from Intuition 1000 Feet Up: Faith Dickey at TEDx-Austin," YouTube video, posted by TEDx Talks, February 19, 2013, https://youtu.be/8zi-yNTOP0s.

"Fear is like": Hannah Summers, "Walking a 3,000-ft Highline with Faith Dickey," *Escapism*, January 28, 2016, https://escapismmagazine.com/features/interview-walking-a-3-000-ft-highline-with-faith-dickey/.

Then the mountains: Faith Dickey, original lyrics, shared via email with author on October 29, 2019, used with permission.

Chapter 3: Melanie Curtis
"Tomorrow I'm jumping.": All quotes are from original author interview with Melanie Curtis on October 24, 2019.

Chapter 4: Bethany Hamilton

I don't need easy: Bethany Hamilton, "I Don't Need Easy," https://bethanyhamilton. com December 6, 2018.

"My fear of losing": Graham Russell, "Bethany Hamilton: 'My Fear of Losing Surfing Was Greater Than My Fear of Sharks,'" *Guardian*, March 6, 2020, https://www. theguardian.com/sport/2020/mar/07/bethany-hamilton-unstoppable-film-my-fear-of-losing-surfing-was-greater-than-my-fear-of-sharks.

"The list of what": Bethany Hamilton, Rick Bundschuh, and Sheryl Berk, *Soul Surfer: A True Story of Faith, Family, and Fighting to Get Back on the Board* (New York: MTV Books, 2004), 108–9.

"If I don't get": Gina Dimuro, "Bethany Hamilton Lost Her Arm to a Shark—Then Got Back on the Surfboard One-Armed," allthatsinteresting.com, August 20, 2018, https://allthatsinteresting.com/bethany-hamilton.

"Did you ever": "How a Young Surfer Who Lost an Arm in a Shark Attack Got Back in the Water," originally aired on *The Oprah Winfrey Show*, February 3, 2004, http://www.oprah.com/own-oprahshow/how-a-young-shark-attack-victim-got-back-in-the-water-video.

"Courage doesn't mean": Bethany Hamilton, *Be Unstoppable: The Art of Never Giving Up* (Grand Rapids, MI: Zondervan, 2018), 75.

Chapter 5: Jill Heinerth

"A really ferocious current": All quotes from original author interview with Jill Heinerth on October 7, 2019, unless otherwise noted here.

"From birth, man": Jacques Cousteau, "Poet of the Depths," *Time*, March 28, 1960.

Chapter 6: Ann Marie Stephens

"That's what I want": All quotes from original author interview with Ann Marie Stephens on January 12, 2020.

Chapter 7: Sneha Sharma

"They were driving": "Giving Flight to My Dreams | Sneha Sharma | TEDxGLIM-Chennai," YouTube video, posted by TEDx Talks, April 4, 2019, https://youtu.be/nKMPUy81gGQ.

"We're here to": "About Us," W Series, accessed September 14, 2020, https://wseries.com/about-us/.

Challenges are the best: "Passion for speed," TEDx GLIMChennai, "Giving Flight to My Dreams," 5:37 timestamp, https://www.youtube.com/watch?v=nKMPUy81gGQ.

"I felt like I was on fire": All quotes from original author interview with Sneha Sharma on December 17, 2019, unless otherwise noted here.

Chapter 8: Elladee Brown

Our goal is": "No Charge for Search and Rescue," FAQ page, British Columbia Search and Rescue Association, January 2014, https://www.bcsara.com/about/faq/no-charge-for-search-and-rescue/.

"Halllooo?": All quotes from original author interview with Elladee Brown on December 6, 2018.

Chapter 9: Lizzie Armanto

"It felt surreal": All quotes from original author interview with Lizzie Armanto on January 27, 2020, unless otherwise noted here.

"Welcome to the": "Lizzie's Pro! Video," YouTube video, uploaded by ThrasherMagazine, March 16, 2017, https://youtu.be/gqT8xesnqvg.

"Hey, Lizzie": "Lizzie Armanto | The Nine Club with Chris Roberts - Episode 168," YouTube video, uploaded by The Nine Club, October 28, 2019, https://youtu.be/ TMj7bgCzsAA.

Lean forward: "The Nine Club with Christ Roberts."

"If you want to": Christine Yu, "A Pro Skateboarder Who's Shredding a Path for Women in the Sport," *Good*, August 7, 2017, https://www.good.is/sports/lizzie-ar-manto-qa.

Chapter 10: Kristin Knight Pace

"Glare ice": All quotes from original author interview with Kristin Knight Pace on November 9, 2019.

Chapter 11: Julia Marino
"Dad, I've got a surprise": All quotes from original author interviews with Julia Marino and John Marino on February 13, 2020, and January 18, 2020, respectively, unless otherwise noted here.

"lead, encourage and support": "Vision and Mission," US Ski and Snowboard Association, accessed September 14, 2020, https://usskiandsnowboard.org/about/ about-more-information.

"Luck is at": "Q&A with Julia Marino," WHEC, November 6, 2017, https://www. whec.com/news/qa-with-julia-marino/4659876/.

Chapter 12: Angela Hawse
"On the mountain it is": All quotes from original author interview with Angela Hawse on December 20, 2019.

Chapter 13: Sara Mudallal

"My name is": Red Bull Jordan, "Meet Sara Mudallal: A Parkour Athlete," Red Bull, September 26, 2018, https://www.redbull.com/mea-en/meet-sara-mudallal-a-parkour-athlete.

"I hope to see": Jordan, "Meet Sara Mudallal."

"Follow your dream": All quotes from original author interview with Sara Mudallal on November 9, 2019, unless otherwise noted here.

"Once you hit": "Fearless Muslim Parkour Athlete," YouTube video, uploaded by Fox 11 Los Angeles, November 7, 2017, https://youtu.be/K9MLeWN19EU.

"I'm actually featured": "Ninja Warrior Experience!!" YouTube video, uploaded by Sara Mudallal, March 14, 2018, https://youtu.be/rz1l6z1OZlU.

"If you're going": "Stickers - Car Max Commercial," YouTube video, uploaded by CarMax, September 30, 2019, https://youtu.be/Zan-YkaWfPo.

You can't stop: "Bebe Rexha - You Can't Stop the Girl (Official Music Video)," YouTube video, uploaded by Bebe Rexha, October 15, 2019, https://youtu.be/1Dm-wyNkmTJ0.

Chapter 14: Brittany Leavitt

"celebrate diversity": Color the Crag, https://www.facebook.com/colorthecrag.

"cutting edge network": "Who We Are," Outdoor Afro, accessed September 14, 2020, https://outdoorafro.com/about/.

"I'm back home": All quotes from original author interview with Brittany Leavitt on December 10, 2019.

Chapter 15: Courtney Dauwalter

"All you have to": "The Ultra Addict with Courtney Dauwalter | Salomon TV," YouTube video, uploaded by Salomon TV, September 10, 2019, https://youtu.be/BbS32MAurnQ.

"There were always multiple": All quotes are from original author interview with Courtney Dauwalter on March 3, 2020, unless otherwise noted here.

"Don't think about": Original author interview with Maggie Guterl on March 16, 2020.